CW00855467

THE GOSPEL OF DECEPTION

AUTHOR OF
COME ON CHURCH! WAKE UP!

THE GOSPEL OF DECEPTION

COUNTERFEIT CHRISTIANITY AND
THE FATE OF ITS FOLLOWERS

MICHELE NEAL

The Gospel of Deception – Counterfeit Christianity and the Fate of its Followers

Copyright © 2017 by Michele Neal.

Graphic design and typesetting by JWC Creative. www.jwccreative.com

No part of this book shall be reproduced or transmitted in any form or by any means, electronic or mechanical, including photocopying, recording, or by any information retrieval system without written permission from the publisher.

For more copies of this book visit www.michelenealuk.com

ISBN: 978-1974387014

Dedication

I dedicate this book to my heavenly Father, His Son Jesus Christ, and to the Holy Spirit.

The message of this book is from The Holy Bible, which is the Word of God. I am simply the hand that He is using to write it.

I would not have written this book unless the Lord had placed within my heart the urgency of His Word concerning the deception that has ensnared His Church in these current times.

My sole purpose in writing it is to obey the Lord in what He has called me to do, which is for His glory alone.

I also dedicate this book in loving memory of my wonderful, joyful dad, David John Cooper, who died on 17th January 2015, suddenly and without warning. I love you, Dad, and I miss you more than words can ever say.

A Voice in the Wilderness

"Then who are you? We need an answer for those who sent us. What do you have to say about yourself?"

John replied in the words of the prophet Isaiah:

*"I am a voice shouting in the wilderness,
'Clear the way for the LORD's coming!'"*

John 1:22-24 NLT

"What I say to you in the dark (privately), tell in the light (publicly); and what you hear whispered in your ear, proclaim from the housetops [to many people]." Matthew 10:27 AMP

Another gospel

"I hope you will put up with a little more of my foolishness. Please bear with me. For I am jealous for you with the jealousy of God himself. I promised you as a pure bride to one husband — Christ. But I fear that somehow your pure and undivided devotion to Christ will be corrupted, just as Eve was deceived by the cunning ways of the serpent. You happily put up with whatever anyone tells you, even if they preach a different Jesus than the one we preach, or a different kind of Spirit than the one you received, or a different kind of gospel than the one you believed." 2 Corinthians 11:1-4 NLT

"I marvel that you are turning away so soon from Him who called you in the grace of Christ, to a different gospel, which is not another; but there are some who trouble you and want to pervert the gospel of Christ. But even if we, or an angel from heaven, preach any other gospel to you than what we have preached to you, let him be accursed. As we have said before, so now I say again, if anyone preaches any other gospel to you than what you have received, let him be accursed.

For do I now persuade men, or God? Or do I seek to please men?

For if I still pleased men, I would not be a bondservant of Christ." Galatians 1:6-10 NKJV

God's Watchman

"Once again a message came to me from the LORD: "Son of man, give your people this message: 'When I bring an army against a country, the people of that land choose one of their own to be a watchman. When the watchman sees the enemy coming, he sounds the alarm to warn the people. Then if those who hear the alarm refuse to take action, it is their own fault if they die. They heard the alarm but ignored it, so the responsibility is theirs. If they had listened to the warning, they could have saved their lives. But if the watchman sees the enemy coming and doesn't sound the alarm to warn the people, he is responsible for their captivity. They will die in their sins, but I will hold the watchman responsible for their deaths.'

"Now, son of man, I am making you a watchman for the people of Israel. Therefore, listen to what I say and warn them for me. If I announce that some wicked people are sure to die and you fail to tell them to change their ways, then they will die in their sins, and I will hold you responsible for their deaths. But if you warn them to repent and they don't repent, they will die in their sins, but you will have saved yourself." Ezekiel 33:1-9 NLT

FOREWORD

The world is changing around us at an astonishing rate, and unfortunately the Church has been tagging along for the ride. Michele Neal is sounding a trumpet blast for all who will hear and heed the warning: it is time to wake up! The Church has been lulled to sleep by the cares of this world and its rapidly changing moral climate. It is time to come out of Babylon lest we be swallowed up by her destruction.

Many great writers and revivalists have written about similar problems in their countries in times past, but something is different today. For the first time, this is not only a British problem. It is not just an American problem. It is not even a Western problem. It is a worldwide phenomenon. And that is new.

That makes the time we are living in that much more critical to pay close attention to. We are in Michele's debt for sounding this alarm and I only pray millions will heed it. I pray you will be changed and challenged by the clarion call to return to the Lord with all your heart.

I pray she will inspire many more authors, speakers and revivalists to join in her call to wake up.

Darren Hibbs - Author of several books including *The year of the Lord's Favor?*; *A Diary of Dreams and Visions* and *Spiritual Gifts: Are They Still For Today?*

ENDORSEMENTS

"A salutary and timely message! Hard hitting, straight to the point and with no holds barred. Meticulously argued and backed up with scripture upon scripture. Warning: This book is not for the itchy-ear Christian! It is for anyone willing to allow the Lord to rebuke, chasten and bring them back to their first love in these last days."

Jason Carter - Author of *Trumpet Blast Warning* and *Beyond Earthly Realms,* and Radio Host of *End Time Hour.*

"Michele has clearly and thoughtfully exposed the counterfeit Christianity that has engulfed the Church today without compromise or excuse. It's refreshing and encouraging to know there are authors who speak the truth found in God's Holy Word. This book will convict many hearts, and it should."

Rev. Jack Munley - Founder and Lead Pastor of Rescue & Restore Church, Olyphant, Pa. Also, hospice chaplain for Home Health Care Professionals and Hospice, and Author of *The Church in America is Dying... But is All Hope Lost?*

ACKNOWLEDGEMENTS

I would like to thank my wonderful husband, Chris, for once again helping me through the long haul of book writing, this one being my third book! When I wrote the first one, I thought that would be my lot! But the Lord compelled me to write a second book... and now a third! I am sure Chris enjoys the long periods of silence whilst I am hidden away in my 'closet' writing the draft manuscripts!

Thank you to my daughter, Emma, for the many hours you have spent proof reading the manuscript and offering your expert advice to get it all into shape. Thank you also to my sister, Sharon, and my mum, Val, for your encouragement during the writing of the manuscript, and your text messages to cheer me on when the going got tough!

Thank you to the many brothers and sisters in Christ whom the Lord has brought into my life, who have encouraged and supported me in this work, and also the many 'followers' around the world on Twitter, who have 'liked' and 're-tweeted' the things I have posted.

A big thank you to three fellow Christian authors for your support and encouragement in the writing of the challenging message of this book, and for your extra help in offering any critical analysis, and in hunting out some of the typos! Firstly to Darren Hibbs, for your kindness and willingness to write the Foreword for this book, and equally to Jason Carter and Rev. Jack Munley for your much-valued endorsements. I really appreciate the time that you have all taken to support me in this way. God bless you all.

Thank you to those at Kingdom Writing Solutions, who have been involved in publishing this book. Your help and support has been much appreciated.

Finally, to my beloved dad, whose soul has left this earth to be with the Lord; thank you for your love and support for the first two books I wrote, and for the words you spoke to me at one of my Testimony Evenings at St. Rhadagund's Christian Centre (Isle of Wight) in August 2014. You said to me, in front of the audience, "You are a voice in the wilderness". Then afterwards, privately, you said to me, "So, another book then?!" These words brought tears to my eyes because you spoke the exact words that the Lord had spoken to me in relation to this book that I am now writing. The Lord said the message of it would be a 'Voice in the Wilderness'.

Two years have passed since you were ripped out of our lives at the start of 2015. It has taken me all this time to push through the grind of daily life without you here. So as we begin the year 2017, I feel that now is the time for this book to be written, for the glory of God, and in memory of you, Dad, and those powerful and significant words, which you spoke to me.

CONTENTS

"The calling of a New Testament worker is to expose sin and to reveal Jesus Christ as Saviour. Consequently, he cannot always be charming and friendly, but must be willing to be stern to accomplish major surgery. We are sent by God to lift up Jesus Christ, not to give wonderfully beautiful speeches. We must be willing to examine others as deeply as God has examined us. We must also be sharply intent on sensing those Scripture passages that will drive the truth home, and then not be afraid to apply them."

Oswald Chambers, *My Utmost for His Highest*, ed. James Reimann (Grand Rapids, MI: Discovery House, 1992) (Excerpt from Dec 20th)

Chapter 1

THE REASON FOR THIS BOOK

This chapter is a vital part of the book, as it sets the scene for the whole purpose of writing it. I have chosen not to call it the 'Introduction' because I know how tempting it can be to skip reading it! Let's view this chapter as the 'Trailer', giving you the desire to want to read to the very end!

But before I start, I would like to tell you a little story, about how this book came to be written.

In June 2014, shortly before my second book, *The End of The World and What Jesus Has to Say About It*, was published, I felt the Lord give me the title for this new book, which you are holding in your hands. I began to write a few scribbled notes, but got sidetracked with the arrival of my parents who were relocating to the area where I live. The manuscript remained untouched for the following six months.

Then, as I mentioned previously in the Dedication and Acknowledgements, my dad died unexpectedly in January 2015. The shock has been so deep that I have not been able to focus on writing this manuscript for the past two years.

In December 2016, I felt an urgent prompting from the Lord to 'get on with it'. I knew what the message was to be about, but I only had a quarter of it written down. The rest of it was a jumbled mess in my head that had been rumbling around for two years and just wouldn't go away.

I decided that I would try to continue the book as soon as 2017 arrived. So, on January 3rd, I sat at my computer and said, "Okay Lord, let's get on with it!"

I began to type what I had already handwritten, but when my notes ran out, I still kept typing! I was stunned at the ease with which the words flowed out of my fingers and on to the keyboard! I felt the Holy Spirit was almost dictating the words to me, and that I was simply His secretary!

Just one week later, the first draft of the manuscript was completed! A further five months have been spent knocking it into shape, proof reading and correcting, and making it ready for submission to the publisher.

All I know is that when God wants something done, He **really does** make it happen, regardless of our natural inabilities! All the glory belongs to Him!

So, let me begin to share with you what is an immense burden in my soul, and which frequently drives me to tears of intercession before the throne of God.

During the past twenty years or so, something has been happening in the Church. Whatever it is, it seemed to start out as a trickle, but has now escalated into a tsunami.

The Church of Jesus Christ is in deep trouble, but by and large it doesn't seem to care. The fact that the Church seems to be deeply apathetic and indifferent to its sickly spiritual condition is a very serious state to be in, especially in the times that we are now living in.

When I became a born-again, Spirit-filled follower of Christ in 1992, the Church, whatever the denomination, generally seemed to have a reverential fear of God's Holiness, His Justice, and the authority of His Word as the truth.

Most churches seemed to know what was right and wrong, in accordance with Holy Scripture, and as such, believers seemed to generally live by the truth of the Word of God, particularly in previous centuries. So when they went astray, the Holy Spirit living in them would prick their conscience, convicting them of their sin, and enabling them to experience godly sorrow for disobeying God's Word. This would enable them to confess and repent of their sin and turn back to God for forgiveness and restoration.

Even as little as twenty years or so ago, outwardly this generally appeared to be the case within the global multi-denominational Church of Jesus Christ. But something has now changed…and it is **not** for the good.

A demonic spirit has crept in unnoticed. This spirit is sitting in our pews, masquerading as an 'angel of light', and is slowly and subtly spreading his evil deception throughout the whole Church, even ascending to the lofty heights of the pulpit.

What is this demonic spirit?

It is the deceiving spirit of 'counterfeit Christianity'; it is a 'Christianity' that practices falsehood, and 'loves to live a lie' (see Revelation 22:15-16).

What do I mean by the term 'counterfeit Christianity'? Well, let's take a valuable painting as an example. A counterfeit painting looks so much like the real painting that even those who are experts in the field of Art can be fooled into believing that the counterfeit painting is the genuine article.

So, with counterfeit Christianity, it can appear and sound **so much** like genuine Christianity, that unless we search the Scriptures to know what is the truth, this counterfeit Christianity will easily deceive us.

As with all counterfeits in life, you have to know and study the **genuine** article in order to detect when a counterfeit is in front of you.

The fact that something of this nature has been happening in the Church in the past twenty years is of grave concern. Alarm bells should be ringing, warning believers to Wake Up! Satan has crept into the Church with a blanket of deception. He has thrown this blanket over the followers of Christ and is smothering them with it, causing them to fall into a state of drowsiness. And in this drowsy state, Satan is allowing his demons to invade the Church with counterfeit doctrine, counterfeit teaching, and counterfeit supernatural manifestations.

All these counterfeits look and sound like authentic Christianity, but they are **not**! The purpose of a counterfeit is to **deceive**.

Counterfeit Christianity is designed to deceive followers of Christ, and lead them away from the absolute and infallible truth of God's Holy Word. This is what Satan wants. He did this in the Garden of Eden. Counterfeit Christianity tries to 'negotiate' with God. In many Churches today, leaders are reading God's Word, then saying "Surely that's not what God really means?" This sounds just like the serpent in the garden, doesn't it? (see Genesis Chapter 3).

Satan has slithered into our churches and is deceiving the minds of our shepherds – our church leaders, who are meant to protect us and watch over our souls, so that we do not get dragged away by 'wolves in sheep's clothing' (see Matthew 7:15).

Sadly, some who were once our uncompromising leaders have now listened to Satan's lies and have been deceived into believing that they can negotiate with God's Holy Word. Our once steadfast leaders have become the very 'wolves in sheep's clothing' that they were supposed to protect us from.

Instead of this raising alarm bells in our spirits, much of the flock is so drowsy that we are following our deceived leaders like 'sheep to the slaughter'. This is "the blind leading the blind, and both fall into the pit" (see Luke 6:39). In the spiritual realm this is not a metaphorical 'pit'; it is the pit of hell, the eternal fire, where

Satan and his demons, and all who follow his lies and deceptions will end up for eternity (see Matthew 25:41).

'Another gospel'

As we will see later in Chapter 4, counterfeit Christianity is the Church preaching 'another gospel'; a watered-down, compromised and altered 'gospel' to suit the times and the culture we are living in. Its outward appearance is very appealing to a growing culture of followers of Christ who now seem to want a gospel of 'anything goes'. In fact, counterfeit Christianity is so appealing to followers of Christ, that Jesus Himself warned us that, in the End Times, these false prophets will be able to deceive even the very elect.

"At that time if anyone says to you, 'Look, here is the Messiah!' or, 'There he is!' do not believe it. For false messiahs and false prophets will appear and perform great signs and wonders to deceive, if possible, even the elect. See, I have told you ahead of time." Matthew 24:23-25 NIV

Counterfeit Christianity has a 'magnetic' appeal, causing people to flock to it, and be swept up in its social and global appeal. People feel invigorated by belonging to this version of 'Christianity' which urges them to cast off the 'chains' of previous centuries of faithful belief, adherence and obedience to God's Word, declaring these things to be nothing but 'religious dogma', old-fashioned, outdated, and no longer relevant to our times. (I will write more on Religious Dogma in Chapter 4 under the sub-heading 'False gospels'.)

Counterfeit Christianity seeks to persuade the Church of today to 'evolve' from what it considers to be 'dated' historical beliefs and teachings, and its goal is to create its own faith and its own 'gospel', but covering its deception by retaining the title of 'Christianity'. In its struggle to usurp authentic Christianity, counterfeit Christianity sets up its own versions to run alongside authentic Christianity, as a new expression of it to 'suit the times'.

I wonder what Jesus feels about this? What must He feel when He sees what His shepherds are doing to His Gospel, and the destruction they are causing to His flock? It must be a pungent stench in His nostrils.

He has made it very clear that all who practice and peddle the evils of falsehood will not be permitted to enter the Kingdom of Heaven (see Revelation 22:14-15). Yet, tragically, the many forms of counterfeit Christianity that are emerging today believe that their 'new gospel' will still save them, and they convince themselves that much of God's Holy Word is no longer correct or valid!

Millions of people are walking, in an almost 'hypnotized' state, along the path of counterfeit Christianity, and the 'Pit of Apostasy' has opened its mouth wide, and is bubbling like a cauldron, ready to receive all who fall into it.

Christians and Christianity once Respected

There was a time when Christians were generally respected, and that was not so long ago. They were considered as people with integrity and morality, who were honourable and trustworthy. But over the years, media reports exposing large scale misconduct, abuse and corruption within religious institutions, which has remained hidden for decades, has caused a turnaround in the way the world views Christians and Christianity.

Where once there was respect towards followers of Christ, there is now at least indifference, but at worst there is open hatred and persecution. They see and hear things about people who profess to be followers of Christ (who are meant to represent Christ upon the earth) committing gross sins and covering them up, hoping that their 'deeds of darkness' will never be found out. But God never allows un-confessed sin to remain hidden. When followers of Christ fail to confess their habitual sins, and also remain unrepentant, in time God always exposes it.

"Remember, the sins of some people are obvious, leading them to certain judgment. But there are others whose sins will not be revealed until later." 1 Timothy 5:24 NLT

When God exposes the sins within His Church, the world must surely see us as a bunch of filthy, disgusting and despicable hypocrites, and that is probably putting it mildly. They see us dishonouring the name of Jesus Christ, and trampling His name in the filth of our unrepentant sins. Is it any wonder that the world has decided that Christians and Christianity are no longer worthy of respect?

Sadly, in the Church's desire to 'resurrect' its previous position of respect in the community and the eyes of the world, it has resorted to compromise. Where once it was respected for its steadfast adherence to the Holy Word of God, the Church is now tearing God's Word to shreds by forsaking His ways and adopting alternative, worldly, man-made views, opinions and practises and labelling them as the new 'Emerging Christianity'. This may cause the world to offer a token of 'respect' towards the Church again, but at what cost to the Church's eternal destiny, when the world's respect for the Church has been gained through its compromise of God's Word?

Forsaking God's Holy Word

Concerning the matter of the Church forsaking God's Word and His ways, let's read the following portion of Scripture taken from Jeremiah 36 (I encourage you to read the whole chapter to get the full impact of this story):

"The king sent Jehudi to get the scroll. Jehudi brought it from Elishama's room and read it to the king as all his officials stood by. It was late autumn, and the king was in a winterized part of the palace, sitting in front of a fire to keep warm. Each time Jehudi finished reading three or four columns, the king took a knife and cut off that section of the scroll. He then threw it into the fire, section by

section, until the whole scroll was burned up. Neither the king nor his attendants showed any signs of fear or repentance at what they heard. Even when Elnathan, Delaiah, and Gemariah begged the king not to burn the scroll, he wouldn't listen." Jeremiah 36:21-26 NLT

This is what the Church of today is doing! By following after and implementing counterfeit teaching, we are saying to God that we no longer want to obey His Holy Word, and so we are effectively ripping it to shreds and burning it in the fire!

The horrendous fate of this king, his descendents, and also his attendants, for refusing to listen to God's warnings, is recorded in Scripture, in Jeremiah 36:27-31. I urge you to read it, as it stands as a dire warning to those who are responsible for God's people.

As followers of Christ, our desire should be to obey God's Word and please Him. Our motives should **not** be to please man, when those things are contrary to God's Word (see Galatians 1:10).

Our mission should be to preach to the world the Gospel message of salvation through faith in Jesus Christ, of God's forgiveness of our sins, and about living our lives in obedience to His Word, which will ultimately result in our souls being saved from eternity in hell so that we can enter the Kingdom of Heaven.

Jesus Himself said,

*"Therefore go and make disciples of all nations, baptizing them in the name of the Father and of the Son and of the Holy Spirit, **and teaching them to obey everything I have commanded you.**"* Matthew 28:19-20(a) NIV (author's emphasis)

Obedience

Obedience to God's Word is what authentic Christianity should be about; not the lukewarm, watered-down, compromising version that is sweeping across the globe today, which turns a blind-eye to God's verdict on sin; and for the sake of love and tolerance, says that it is okay for believers to remain as they are, in their unrepentant sin, and condones their behaviour with the comforting platitude of, "It's okay because God loves them!"

Yes, God does love them as human beings because He created them and does not want anyone to perish, but His desire is that all would come to repentance (see 2 Peter 3:9). But it comes down to this: God hates sin so much that He sent His son, Jesus Christ, to die on the cross and shed His blood, to take upon Himself the full punishment of all our sins. He did this to make it possible for the whole human race to receive God's forgiveness of our sins, and salvation from eternity in hell… But we have got to **accept** this truth and believe in, follow and **obey** Jesus. If we claim we are a follower of Christ, obedience to the Word of God is **not** an optional extra!

With this knowledge, why on earth would the Church think it is okay for followers of Christ to carry on living lives of sin?

But more importantly, why would the Church think that **God** is okay with us continuing to sin, and remaining unrepentant about it? The Church today has been, and is being seriously deceived by the 'god of this world' (see 2 Corinthians 4:4).

In the following passage taken from his classic devotional, *My Utmost for His Highest,* Oswald Chambers gives us a serious message about the subject of sin in the lives of followers of Christ.

"Complete And Effective Decision About Sin"

"…our old man was crucified with Him, that the body of sin might be done away with, that we should no longer be slaves of sin" Romans 6:6

Co- Crucifixion. Have you made the following decision about sin – that it must be completely killed in you? It takes a long time to come to this complete and effective decision about sin. It is, however, the greatest moment in your life once you decide that sin must die in you – not simply be restrained, suppressed or counteracted, but crucified

– just as Christ died for the sin of the world. No one can bring anyone to this decision. We may be mentally and spiritually convinced, but what we need to do is actually make the decision that Paul urged us to do in this passage. Pull yourself up, take some time alone with God, and make this important decision, saying, "Lord, identify me with your death until I know that sin has died in me." Make the moral decision that sin in you must be put to death.

This was not some divine future experience on the part of Paul, but was a very radical and definite experience in his life. Are you prepared to let the Spirit of God search you until you know what the level and nature of sin is in your life – to see the very things that struggle against God's Spirit in you? If so, will you then agree with God's verdict on the nature of sin – that it should be identified with the death of Jesus? You cannot "reckon yourselves to be dead indeed to sin" (6:11) unless you have radically dealt with the issue of your will before God.

Have you entered into the glorious privilege of being crucified with Christ, until all that remains in your flesh and blood is His life? "I have been crucified with Christ; it is no longer I who live, but Christ lives in me..." (Galatians 2:20)

(Whole passage entry April 10th) [1]

This is a very clear message to the Church, but sadly, it is even clearer that the Church is paying absolutely no attention!

Satan has swooped into the Church under the cloak of 'tolerance', deceiving church leaders with the lie that says, "As God is a 'God of love', it is part of His loving nature to allow people to carry on doing whatever pleases them."

The further that professing Christians are led away from obeying God's Word, and the more they are permitted to remain in their sinful lifestyles, the easier it becomes for Satan to cause them to believe his counterfeit doctrines and counterfeit teachings. He doesn't do this in big and obvious ways because followers of

Christ would spot his deceptive activity a mile off, and they would immediately reject it!

Satan is not stupid! He knows how to deceive those who say they are followers of Christ. All Satan has to do is subtly twist God's Word here and there, and repackage it to make this 'twisted word' sound like God's truth.

Satan is targeting his deception at the shepherds; the leaders of the Church, who are falling for his counterfeits like ninepins in a bowling alley. The leaders believe these 'lovely-sounding' lies, and then feed these counterfeits to the sheep, who gobble up these 'poisons' and swallow them whole.

What started out as a trickle has now turned into a flood. The Church has opened its doors wide, and is saying to the enemy, "Oh, how lovely of you to join us! Do come in! You are most welcome! Do find a comfortable seat and make yourself at home among us!"

Come on Church! Wake Up! … What are we doing?

Apostasy – From the Pulpit to the Pews

God's Word is **clear** on what is right and what is wrong. His Word is holy, righteous and just, and He has given us clear warnings of the consequences we will face now and in eternity, when we disobey and rebel against His Holy Word.

The Church is on the brink of disaster. It is wobbling precariously on a knife-edge, teetering on the edge of the abyss. If it does not wake up **urgently**, Jesus will snuff it out (see Revelation 2:5).

The Church is in perilous times. Jesus warned of a deception that would invade the Church during the End Times, leading believers to fall away from the truth, which we will see later in Chapters 2 and 4.

Read this severe warning, which God gave to His Prophet Malachi, to deliver to God's Spiritual leaders at that time. It stands out as a beacon of warning to the whole of the global Church today.

"Listen, you priests — this command is for you! Listen to me and make up your minds to honor my name," says the LORD of Heaven's Armies, "or I will bring a terrible curse against you. I will curse even the blessings you receive. Indeed, I have already cursed them, because you have not taken my warning to heart. I will punish your descendants and splatter your faces with the manure from your festival sacrifices, and I will throw you on the manure pile. Then at last you will know it was I who sent you this warning so that my covenant with the Levites can continue," says the LORD of Heaven's Armies.

"The purpose of my covenant with the Levites was to bring life and peace, and that is what I gave them. This required reverence from them, and they greatly revered me and stood in awe of my name. They passed on to the people the truth of the instructions they received from me. They did not lie or cheat; they walked with me, living good and righteous lives, and they turned many from lives of sin.

"The words of a priest's lips should preserve knowledge of God, and people should go to him for instruction, for the priest is the messenger of the LORD of Heaven's Armies. But you priests have left God's paths. Your instructions have caused many to stumble into sin. You have corrupted the covenant I made with the Levites," says the LORD of Heaven's Armies. "So I have made you despised and humiliated in the eyes of all the people. For you have not obeyed me but have shown favoritism in the way you carry out my instructions." Malachi 2:1-9 NLT

Equally, the apostle Paul warns believers,

"The wrath of God is being revealed from heaven against all the **godlessness and wickedness of people, who suppress the truth by their wickedness..."** Romans 1:18a NIV (author's emphasis)

Counterfeit Christianity is now running rampant throughout the Church, and the sheep are falling away from the truth in astronomical numbers. We want a cosy kind of 'Christianity' that comforts us but does not convict us; soothes us but does not shake us. We want to be saved but still sin; cry but not confess; rejoice but not repent.

This kind of Christianity is **counterfeit Christianity**. Measure it with the truth of God's Word and you will see how utterly deceptive and devoid of God's authority our modern-day 'Christianity' really is. We are living in a time where many of our churches are being lead by pastors, ministers, vicars and priests who refuse to submit to the authority of God's Word, and we are listening to and believing the deceptions that they preach.

Surely we must be able to see that what is happening in the Church indicates that we are in the times of the 'End Times' Apostasy ... the great 'falling away'.

Apostasy does not just mean falling away from the faith and becoming an atheist. Apostasy also mean a falling away from believing and obeying the truth of God's Word, and instead, believing and following a counterfeit Christianity, yet **still** claiming and professing that we are a follower of Christ.

The reason for this book is to expose counterfeit Christianity. In the following chapters, we will look at what Jesus said about it in the Gospels, and what the apostles said. We will also highlight what some of the varying forms of counterfeit Christianity look like in the Church today.

We will look at what God's Word says will be the fate of all who believe and follow false doctrine and false teachings. Then we will end this book with an offer of hope to all who want to be free from counterfeit Christianity.

Jesus is coming back for a Church that is faithfully following and obeying the truth of God's Word. He will not receive a Bride who has rejected His Word and is following a counterfeit.

"Write This in the Book!"

Recently, whilst in the process of writing this manuscript, I struggled to fall asleep one night. I was very restless, and I tossed and turned for ages. My mind just would not settle, but I didn't know what the problem was. So I prayed and asked the Lord if there was anything He wanted to say to me.

Instantly I felt the Lord say, "Write this in the book." I switched my bedside light on and fumbled about for my note pad and pen, and then began to write. What I wrote was in the prophetic style of the Lord speaking to followers of Christ who are sinning, and are unrepentant. Below is the message, which flowed out of my pen and onto the paper in the early hours of the morning.

A Message from the Bridegroom

"On the day you gave your life to Me, I forgave you of the sins of your past and washed you clean, so that you could start living your new life in Me, without spot or blemish. I clothed you in a clean, pure white wedding garment, as one who is betrothed to Me. But you must keep your garment clean and pure through confession and repentance of your daily sins.

"Does My Word not tell you in 1 John 1:8 that if you say you have no sin, then you are deceiving yourself? Does My Word not also say in 1 John 1:9 that **if** you confess your sins, I am faithful and just to forgive you of your sins and cleanse you from your unrighteousness? I will do this for you if you confess and repent.

"But if you deliberately keep on sinning and disobeying My Word, whilst still saying you are My follower, this Word that you refuse to obey also tells you in Hebrews 10:26-27 that there is no longer any sacrifice that will cover your unrepentant sins. There is only the terrible expectation of God's judgment and the raging fire that will consume His enemies.

"If you fail to keep your wedding garment clean through daily confession and repentance, on the Day of Judgment I will see your filthy wedding garment, and I will remove it from you as one who is not worthy to wear it or to be joined with Me as My Bride.

"My Word says in Revelation 22:15 that you will be left outside the Kingdom of Heaven, walking around naked and ashamed. This is because I will have removed the wedding garment, which I gave to you when you first believed in Me; when your love for Me was so great that obedience to My Word was your delight.

"But if your love for Me has grown cold whilst you have been waiting for Me to return, and you have been drawn aside into following the counterfeit teachings of false prophets who I warned you to avoid, and you have not kept your wedding garment clean by repenting; if I find you like this on the Day of Judgment, then My Word will stand as your judge. Be warned My child…Repent, for the time is short."

Indeed, the time appears to be very short.

Come on Church, Wake up!

Chapter 2

WHAT JESUS HAS TO SAY

Jesus does not use the words 'counterfeit Christianity' in the Gospels, but He does use the words 'false prophets' in relation to counterfeit preachers of the Gospel, and 'false messiahs' or 'false Christs' in relation to those proclaiming to be Himself.

He knew these things would be coming upon the earth and into the Church, and so He warned His followers about it in advance, exhorting them to be watchful and ready for it so that they would not be caught out and deceived. So let's turn to the Gospels to read what Jesus spoke and taught regarding this serious subject.

Jesus was speaking to His disciples concerning the end times and they asked Him,

"Tell us, when will all this happen? What sign will signal your return and the end of the world?"

Jesus told them, "Don't let anyone mislead you, for many will come in my name, claiming, 'I am the Messiah.' They will deceive many." Matthew 24:4-5 & Mark 13:4-6 NLT

Again, Jesus warns them,

"Then if anyone tells you, 'Look, here is the Messiah,' or 'There he is,' don't believe it. For false messiahs and false prophets will rise up and perform great signs and wonders so as to deceive, if possible, even God's chosen ones. See, I have warned you about this ahead of time. "So if someone tells you, 'Look, the Messiah is out in the desert,' don't

bother to go and look. Or, 'Look, he is hiding here,' don't believe it! For as the lightning flashes in the east and shines to the west, so it will be when the Son of Man comes." Matthew 24:23-27 NLT

"And then if any man shall say to you, Lo, here is Christ; or, lo, he is there; believe him not: For false Christs and false prophets shall rise, and shall shew signs and wonders, to seduce, if it were possible, even the elect. But take ye heed: behold, I have foretold you all things." Mark 13:21-23 KJV

"And many false prophets shall rise, and shall deceive many." Matthew 24:11 KJV

Having read these scriptures, which are the words of Jesus Himself, we cannot be in any doubt that He is warning His followers to be on the lookout for counterfeit Christianity, and to be on guard against it insidiously creeping into the Church to deceive the flock. Jesus' warnings are as clear as a trumpet blast to the Church, but are we listening? Are we paying attention?

A Deadly Slumber

With the state the Church is in at this present time, it would seem that the Church has fallen asleep whilst on watch, the enemy has gained entry into the Temple of God, and is wreaking havoc with its 'delicious-sounding' but nevertheless **evil** fruit of false teaching and 'other gospels'.

The Church has eaten of this 'forbidden fruit', laced with enough 'poison' to cause us to become so deceived by the 'delicacies' that counterfeit Christianity has to offer, that we are willing to walk on Satan's wide path which will lead us to destruction. Not only are some churches willing to walk on this wide path, it appears that many are joyfully doing so, and are encouraging others to do the same!

This is shocking! What on earth are we doing?! Jesus has warned us **not** to follow these counterfeits, so why are we doing this? Why are we ignoring the One who has **warned** us not to follow these things? This is the Son of God Whom we are ignoring! Have we no fear of God's Holiness and justice? Do we think we can just ignore what Jesus says, without there being any consequences to our disobedience and rebellion?

Do we think we can just 'conveniently' blot out large portions of Holy Scripture spoken by the Son of God, and insert our own 'new doctrine' in its place to suit our preferred version of 'Christianity'; teachings which allow us to live, without any conscience, the kind of life that is **contrary** to God's Holy Word?

If we listen to and believe Satan's counterfeits, and eat the forbidden fruit that Jesus has warned us not to partake of, and if we do not confess and repent, there will be consequences to us, physically and spiritually, both now and in eternity.

As it was for Adam and Eve in the Garden of Eden (see Genesis Chapter 3), so it will be for us. We are not exempt from God's justice, and we are deceived if we think otherwise. We cannot habitually disobey and rebel against God's Word and expect all to continue to go well for us.

Jesus says there is an eternal price to pay for rebellion and rejecting His Word. The Bible says that "rebellion is as witchcraft" (see 1 Samuel 15:23), and all who practice it will not inherit the Kingdom of God, and their eternal fate is in the fiery lake of burning sulphur (see Galatians 5:20-12 & Revelation 21:8). **This** is the Word of God.

With that in mind, are we, the Church, still going to ignore the warnings of Jesus Christ, the Messiah, the One we profess to follow? Or are we going to humble ourselves before the throne of God, and confess and repent of our sins, and receive His forgiveness and restoration?

Jesus is pleading with His Bride to wake up from this devastating slumber of deception, and rid herself of the sin of believing and following a counterfeit Christianity, which has ensnared her with its lies, and is dragging her away to destruction.

The Bride of Christ, or the bride of Satan?

The trouble is that the Bride of Christ has forsaken her faithfulness to her Bridegroom (Jesus) and has fallen in love with the enemy (Satan). The enemy has tempted her away from faithful obedience to her Beloved, and has enticed her to partake of the fruits of unrighteousness.

Satan has made these 'fruits' taste sweet and juicy. He is whispering into the Church's ears saying, "These are lovely! They are good for you! They will increase your flock! They will give you credibility with the world! This will increase your profile, and people will seek you for knowledge of your 'new revelations' of God's Word! Surely you must desire this fruit?"

Doesn't Satan's whisperings sound like music to our 'itching ears' (see 2 Timothy 4:3)? Nevertheless, his whisperings are **lies** from the pit of hell! When 'new revelations' are contrary to what is written in the Word of God, they are counterfeit revelations. They are false gospels containing false doctrine.

However, it is clear in both the Old and New Testaments that God does give His faithful followers dreams and visions, and prophetic revelations about His already written Word, but He never gives us 'new revelations' which are contrary to it.

All such suggestions to put a new interpretation or a new spin on God's Word, which undermines God's authority, and encourages and entices followers of Christ to **question** God's already written Holy Word, and to re-write Scripture for themselves to suit the beliefs of their 'new revelations', are the works of Darkness; the lies of Satan.

Jesus said, "You shall know the truth, and the truth shall set you free" (see John 8:32). We must flee from Satan's lies, get back

34

to the truth of God's Word, and **obey** it. Only then will we be free. Following Satan's subtle lies will slowly entangle us in his web of deception…from which there will be no escape if we fail to confess and repent **before** Jesus returns.

This is why Jesus warns us so strongly to be alert and on our guard for these 'wolves in sheep's clothing' (see Matthew 7:15). If there were not any consequences to us following any 'wind of doctrine' (see Ephesians 4:14) that takes our fancy, Jesus would not have bothered to warn us.

We must get back to basics. Return to and obey what we first heard and believed (see Revelation 3:3).

Jesus is coming back for a pure, holy and spotless Bride, washed clean with the water of His Word (see Ephesians 5:25(b) - 27), not a bride covered with the filth and stench of habitual and unrepentant sins that make her indistinguishable from the world of unbelievers.

Come on Church! Wake Up!

Chapter 3

WHAT THE APOSTLES SAID

Having seen what Jesus has to say about counterfeit Christianity, in the guise of false prophets and false messiahs infiltrating the Church, let's now take a look at what the apostles have to say on this subject.

It is important to note that the apostles spent all their time with Jesus during His three-year ministry leading up to His crucifixion, and including His resurrection and ascension into heaven.

Being followers of Jesus, one would assume that what He taught them would have sunk into their hearts and had an impact on their lives. Let's see if this is the case and what we can discern by looking at some Scriptures throughout the apostles' letters and epistles.

Paul's Warnings

The apostle Paul, speaking to the disciples at Ephesus, knowing that his time on earth was nearing its end, said to them,

"And now I know that none of you to whom I have preached the Kingdom will ever see me again. I declare today that I have been faithful. If anyone suffers eternal death, it's not my fault, for I didn't shrink from declaring all that God wants you to know.

"So guard yourselves and God's people. Feed and shepherd God's flock — his church, purchased with his own blood—over which the Holy Spirit has appointed you as leaders. I know that false teachers, like vicious wolves, will come in among you after I leave, not sparing

the flock. Even some men from your own group will rise up and distort the truth in order to draw a following. Watch out! Remember the three years I was with you —my constant watch and care over you night and day, and my many tears for you." Acts 20:25-31 NLT

Again, Paul, speaking to the believers in Galatia says,

"Have I now become your enemy because I am telling you the truth?

Those false teachers are so eager to win your favor, but their intentions are not good. They are trying to shut you off from me so that you will pay attention only to them." Galatians 4:16-18 NLT

Paul says to Timothy,

"Now the Holy Spirit tells us clearly that in the last times some will turn away from the true faith; they will follow deceptive spirits and teachings that come from demons. These people are hypocrites and liars, and their consciences are dead." 1 Timothy 4:1-2 NLT

The Fate of False Teachers, and All Who Follow Them

Next, the apostle Peter gives a long, detailed and shocking warning concerning false teachers, and the fate of all who follow their deception.

"But there were also false prophets in Israel, just as there will be false teachers among you. They will cleverly teach destructive heresies and even deny the Master who bought them. In this way, they will bring sudden destruction on themselves. Many will follow their evil teaching and shameful immorality. And because of these teachers, the way of truth will be slandered. In their greed they will make up clever lies to get hold of your money. But God condemned them long ago, and their destruction will not be delayed.

For God did not spare even the angels who sinned. He threw them into hell, in gloomy pits of darkness, where they are being held until the day of judgment. And God did not spare the ancient world —

except for Noah and the seven others in his family. Noah warned the world of God's righteous judgment. So God protected Noah when he destroyed the world of ungodly people with a vast flood. Later, God condemned the cities of Sodom and Gomorrah and turned them into heaps of ashes. He made them an example of what will happen to ungodly people. But God also rescued Lot out of Sodom because he was a righteous man who was sick of the shameful immorality of the wicked people around him. Yes, Lot was a righteous man who was tormented in his soul by the wickedness he saw and heard day after day. So you see, the Lord knows how to rescue godly people from their trials, even while keeping the wicked under punishment until the day of final judgment. He is especially hard on those who follow their own twisted sexual desire, and who despise authority.

These people are proud and arrogant, daring even to scoff at supernatural beings without so much as trembling. But the angels, who are far greater in power and strength, do not dare to bring from the Lord a charge of blasphemy against those supernatural beings.

These false teachers are like unthinking animals, creatures of instinct, born to be caught and destroyed. They scoff at things they do not understand, and like animals, they will be destroyed. Their destruction is their reward for the harm they have done. They love to indulge in evil pleasures in broad daylight. They are a disgrace and a stain among you. They delight in deception even as they eat with you in your fellowship meals. They commit adultery with their eyes, and their desire for sin is never satisfied. They lure unstable people into sin, and they are well trained in greed. They live under God's curse. They have wandered off the right road and followed the footsteps of Balaam son of Beor, who loved to earn money by doing wrong. But Balaam was stopped from his mad course when his donkey rebuked him with a human voice.

These people are as useless as dried-up springs or as mist blown away by the wind. They are doomed to blackest darkness. They brag about themselves with empty, foolish boasting. With an appeal to twisted sexual desires, they lure back into sin those who have barely escaped from a lifestyle of deception. They promise freedom, but they themselves are slaves of sin and corruption. For you are a slave to whatever controls you. And when people escape from the wickedness of the world by knowing our Lord and Savior Jesus Christ and then get tangled up and enslaved by sin again, they are worse off than before. It would be better if they had never known the way to righteousness than to know it and then reject the command they were given to live a holy life. They prove the truth of this proverb: "A dog returns to its vomit." And another says, "A washed pig returns to the mud." 2 Peter 2:1-22 NLT

Jude Gives a Similar Warning

"Dear friends, I had been eagerly planning to write to you about the salvation we all share. But now I find that I must write about something else, urging you to defend the faith that God has entrusted once for all time to his holy people. I say this because some ungodly people have wormed their way into your churches, saying that God's marvelous grace allows us to live immoral lives. The condemnation of such people was recorded long ago, for they have denied our only Master and Lord, Jesus Christ.

So I want to remind you, though you already know these things, that Jesus first rescued the nation of Israel from Egypt, but later he destroyed those who did not remain faithful. And I remind you of the angels who did not stay within the limits of authority God gave them but left the place where they belonged. God has kept them securely chained in prisons of darkness, waiting for the great day of judgment. And don't forget Sodom and Gomorrah and their neighboring towns, which were filled with immorality and every kind of sexual perversion. Those cities were destroyed by fire and serve as a warning of the eternal fire of God's judgment.

In the same way, these people — who claim authority from their dreams — live immoral lives, defy authority, and scoff at supernatural

40

beings. But even Michael, one of the mightiest of the angels, did not dare accuse the devil of blasphemy, but simply said, "The Lord rebuke you!" (This took place when Michael was arguing with the devil about Moses' body.) But these people scoff at things they do not understand. Like unthinking animals, they do whatever their instincts tell them, and so they bring about their own destruction. What sorrow awaits them! For they follow in the footsteps of Cain, who killed his brother. Like Balaam, they deceive people for money. And like Korah, they perish in their rebellion.

When these people eat with you in your fellowship meals commemorating the Lord's love, they are like dangerous reefs that can shipwreck you. They are like shameless shepherds who care only for themselves. They are like clouds blowing over the land without giving any rain. They are like trees in autumn that are doubly dead, for they bear no fruit and have been pulled up by the roots. They are like wild waves of the sea, churning up the foam of their shameful deeds. They are like wandering stars, doomed forever to blackest darkness.

Enoch, who lived in the seventh generation after Adam, prophesied about these people. He said, "Listen! The Lord is coming with countless thousands of his holy ones to execute judgment on the people of the world. He will convict every person of all the ungodly things they have done and for all the insults that ungodly sinners have spoken against him." These people are grumblers and complainers, living only to satisfy their desires. They brag loudly about themselves, and they flatter others to get what they want.

But you, my dear friends, must remember what the apostles of our Lord Jesus Christ predicted. They told you that in the last times there would be scoffers whose purpose in life is to satisfy their ungodly desires. These people are the ones who are creating divisions among you. They follow their natural instincts because they do not have God's Spirit in them.

But you, dear friends, must build each other up in your most holy faith, pray in the power of the Holy Spirit, and await the mercy of our

Lord Jesus Christ, who will bring you eternal life. In this way, you will keep yourselves safe in God's love.

And you must show mercy to those whose faith is wavering. Rescue others by snatching them from the flames of judgment. Show mercy to still others, but do so with great caution, hating the sins that contaminate their lives." Jude 3-23 NLT

The Apostle John's Warning about False Prophets

"Dear friends, do not believe everyone who claims to speak by the Spirit. You must test them to see if the spirit they have comes from God. For there are many false prophets in the world. This is how we know if they have the Spirit of God: If a person claiming to be a prophet acknowledges that Jesus Christ came in a real body, that person has the Spirit of God. But if someone claims to be a prophet and does not acknowledge the truth about Jesus, that person is not from God. Such a person has the spirit of the Antichrist, which you heard is coming into the world and indeed is already here." 1 John 4:1-4 NLT

Are we Paying Attention?

We can see from all these Scriptures that the apostles paid great attention to what Jesus warned them concerning counterfeit Christianity worming its way into their midst. We should not be surprised at all that these passages written by the apostles confirm and uphold Jesus' Word. The apostles were followers of Christ, and Scripture tells us in Matthew 10:24 that a servant is not above his master.

As such, our preaching and teaching should likewise confirm and uphold the teachings of our Master, Jesus Christ. If our teaching is different and contrary to His Word, then we can be sure that we are teaching, preaching, believing and following a counterfeit Christianity.

What the apostles say in these passages of Scripture is written to teach and exhort **all** believers throughout all generations until Jesus returns, to be watchful for the arrival of these 'wolves in sheep's clothing', and instead of welcoming them into our midst, we should be commanding them to flee in Jesus' name!

Simon, the Sorcerer

The story of Simon the Sorcerer, from the Book of Acts, is a perfect example of someone displaying the characteristics of counterfeit Christianity. He was previously not a follower of Christ, but because of the things he did to astound the people with his sorcery, the people considered him to be 'the Great One – the Power of God', and Simon himself even claimed to be someone great! But he then heard the Gospel, and he believed and got baptised. So, naturally, we would now accept that he was a follower of Christ.

Let's have a look at this passage to see what happens.

"A man named Simon had been a sorcerer there for many years, amazing the people of Samaria and claiming to be someone great. Everyone, from the least to the greatest, often spoke of him as "the Great One — the Power of God." They listened closely to him because for a long time he had astounded them with his magic.

But now the people believed Philip's message of Good News concerning the Kingdom of God and the name of Jesus Christ. As a result, many men and women were baptized. Then Simon himself believed and was baptized. He began following Philip wherever he went, and he was amazed by the signs and great miracles Philip performed.

When the apostles in Jerusalem heard that the people of Samaria had accepted God's message, they sent Peter and John there. As soon as they arrived, they prayed for these new believers to receive the Holy Spirit. The Holy Spirit had not yet come upon any of them, for they had only been baptized in the name of the Lord Jesus. Then Peter and John laid their hands upon these believers, and they received the Holy Spirit.

When Simon saw that the Spirit was given when the apostles laid their hands on people, he offered them money to buy this power. "Let me have this power, too," he exclaimed, "so that when I lay my hands on people, they will receive the Holy Spirit!"

But Peter replied, "May your money be destroyed with you for thinking God's gift can be bought! You can have no part in this, for your heart is not right with God. Repent of your wickedness and pray to the Lord. Perhaps he will forgive your evil thoughts, for I can see that you are full of bitter jealousy and are held captive by sin."

"Pray to the Lord for me," Simon exclaimed, "that these terrible things you've said won't happen to me!" Acts 8:9-24 NLT

Here we have a man previously caught up in the occult, who, after hearing the Gospel preached and getting baptised, outwardly appears to have become a follower of Christ. Peter and John then arrive to pray for the people who have accepted the Gospel and been baptised, to be filled with the Holy Spirit. Simon sees these other believers being filled with the Holy Spirit when the apostles laid their hands on them.

All of a sudden, Simon is consumed with a desire to manifest the power to fill people with the Holy Spirit, probably because of his previous ability to do all sorts of 'astounding things' with his sorcery. It's almost as if he thinks that being filled with the Holy Spirit is just another 'trick' he can add to his list!

So Simon tries to bribe the apostles to give him this power, by offering them money! Peter's response is full of wisdom and the authority of God. He rebukes Simon for his wickedness and tells him that he can have no part in this, and that his heart is not right with God.

Peter tells him to **repent** of his wickedness and pray to God that **perhaps** He would forgive him of his evil thoughts. It is clear here that God will only forgive us if we repent of our sins, but interestingly, Peter's response to Simon seems to suggest that Simon's sin is so great that even if he repents of it, only **perhaps** God may forgive him! Simon is so shocked by what Peter says that he asks Peter to pray to the Lord for him that these terrible things would not happen to him.

Clearly, Simon had grieved the Holy Spirit and was in danger of perishing, despite believing the Gospel and being baptised. Any abuse of the Holy Spirit is an extremely serious matter in the sight of God. We cannot conjure up or magically create manifestations of the Holy Spirit. This is bordering on sorcery (witchcraft). Satan can create counterfeit manifestations to trick and deceive us, like Simon did before Philip arrived and preached the Gospel.

Whoever comes our way displaying 'signs and wonders' or preaching 'another gospel', no matter how well known that person is, or how good their 'Christian credentials' may be, if they are preaching, teaching or doing **anything** that is a deviation from the authority of the Holy Word of God, then their 'message' is a deception. Their 'gospel' is a counterfeit of the authentic truth of God's Word.

So, as Jesus warned His first followers about counterfeit Christianity, and the apostles have also warned us about it, in the next chapter let's have a look at some examples of what 'counterfeit Christianity' looks like in the twenty-first century.

Remember, a counterfeit has the appearance of being the genuine article, but there will be subtle flaws, which are only detectable on very close and thorough examination.

The tool to measure whether a church or ministry's preaching and teaching is a counterfeit is to hold it up to the light of The Bible and see how it compares. Any area of its preaching and teaching that deviates from Holy Scripture is a sure sign that that church or ministry has compromised its beliefs at some point. Once they have opened the door to false teaching, through compromise on any point, they have in effect 'opened the floodgates', and every form of spiritual deception will begin to present itself to them, and will subtly and gradually erode their adherence and obedience to the authority of God's Word.

Satan will 'corner' them over specific Scriptures, particularly moral ones, saying to them, "Did God really say that?" (see Genesis 3:1). They will begin to question God's Holy Word, just like Adam and Eve did.

The Garden of Eden

Adam was the spiritual head (the leader) over Eve. Pastors, priests, vicars, and **any** church leaders are the Spiritual heads over their congregations.

Adam stood by and **allowed** Satan to deceive Eve, and he watched her eat the forbidden fruit. Not only that, Adam **joined** her in believing Satan's deception and then he also ate the fruit that God had strictly forbidden them to eat.

There are Church leaders all over the world who are doing what Adam did. They are allowing Satan to cause them to question the very Word of God. They are allowing Satan to twist Holy Scripture; they then believe his 'version' of God's Word, and are encouraging their flock to believe it too. Seemingly without the slightest conscience, like Adam, our spiritual heads are then standing by and allowing those in their care to eat this 'forbidden fruit'.

Our leaders are calling Satan's lies a 'new revelation of God's Word', which they want to embrace and feed to a new generation of believers. These 'new teachings' may appear 'godly', but are nevertheless a twisted distortion of God's Word.

The Church around the world is now full of sickly sheep, who are in the care of even more sickly shepherds. They have swallowed Satan's bait and are gradually being poisoned by the fruit that God **forbade** them to consume.

So in the next chapter, let's now look at Satan's counterfeits to authentic, Biblical Christianity.

Chapter 4

SATAN'S COUNTERFEITS

End Times Deception and the Great Apostasy

This is a large chapter, but I have done the best I can to break it down into readable sections relating to the various versions of counterfeit Christianity that are currently enticing believers to follow.

As we have already read in the previous chapters, both Jesus and the apostles warned believers to be on the lookout for the appearance of counterfeits. So in this chapter we are going to highlight some modern-day examples. Much of the information is available to read in the public domain, and for the variety of the headings and sub-headings below, and the content of those sections, the sources I have used are:

www.olivetreenews.org
www.breakingisraelnews.com
www.endtimeheadlines.org
www.lighthousetrailsresearch.com
www.charismanews.com
www.standforthetruth.com

Because I have listed these sources here, I will not repeat them again in the various headings. You can search online for the things I mention, as they are freely available for all to discover.

But before we proceed, I would just like to mention that before I became a follower of Christ, I was caught up in many things which, in hindsight, I wish I had never done. What is even more distressing to me is that, after I became a follower of Christ in 1992, I allowed myself to become deceived and got caught up in many of Satan's counterfeits.

Through the many wrong choices I have made in my life in Christ, my growth in faith suffered many setbacks over the years. But thankfully, in October 2011, God, in His great mercy, reached down and extended His hand of grace and love to me, and showed me exactly what my un-confessed and unrepentant sins look like in His sight.

This was a gruelling experience, which took me through a very painful period of godly sorrow, leading to confession and repentance. What God showed me, and what He took me through has changed my life, and what He continues to reveal to me helps to keep me at His feet.

I share this with you so that you will understand that I personally know what it is like, as a follower of Christ, to be caught up in things that we are convinced are not a deception.

On that note, let us now look at some of the things the Lord has revealed to me about Satan's counterfeits, since God powerfully invaded my 'life of deception' in October 2011.

i) False gospels

Where do I begin with this category? There are so many counterfeits being portrayed as modern or 'emerging' Christianity, that they would probably fill a whole separate book to expose them all! That is not the purpose of this chapter, but I will highlight a few, and leave you to do a search for others.

Universalism

The deception of this 'gospel' is that its teaching is that all will be saved, whether we sin or not, and whatever we believe or don't believe. Let's make one thing absolutely clear: salvation and eternal life in heaven are **not** our automatic inheritance, regardless of what beliefs we hold or don't hold, or whatever religion we may follow.

Salvation and eternal life are the promised inheritance of all who believe in and have faith in the One who died on the Cross, to set them free from sin and eternal punishment in hell (see John 3:16).

The One who did this, for the whole human race throughout the whole world, is Jesus Christ, Who is the Messiah (see Matthew 16:16). The complete work of salvation is finished; it happened at Calvary, on the Cross, where Jesus was crucified (see John Chapter 19). From that point on, salvation was and has been made **available** for all, no matter who we are or where we come from; but again I stress that inheriting eternal life is **not** our 'automatic right'. In order to receive this free gift of salvation and eternal life, we must believe in, have faith in, and follow and obey Jesus Christ, the One who gave His life for us.

In the Amplified Bible, the apostle John says,

"For God so [greatly] loved and dearly prized the world, that He [even] gave His [One and] only begotten Son, so that whoever believes and trusts in Him [as Savior] shall not perish, but have eternal life. For God did not send the Son into the world to judge and condemn the world [that is, to initiate the final judgment of the world], but that the world might be saved through Him. Whoever believes and has decided to trust in Him [as personal Savior and Lord] is not judged [for this one, there is no judgment, no rejection, no condemnation]; but the one who does not believe [and has decided to reject Him as personal Savior and Lord] is judged already [that one has been convicted and sentenced], because he has not believed and trusted in the name of the [One and] only begotten Son of God [the One who is truly unique, the only One of His kind, the One who alone can save him]. This is the judgment [that is, the cause for indictment, the test

by which people are judged, the basis for the sentence]: the Light has come into the world, and people loved the darkness rather than the Light, for their deeds were evil. For every wrongdoer hates the Light, and does not come to the Light [but shrinks from it] for fear that his [sinful, worthless] activities will be exposed and condemned. John 3:16-20 AMP

Salvation is through no other (see Acts 4:11-12). As the above Scripture clearly shows, if I do not believe or I refuse to accept God's gift to me through faith in Jesus, I am condemned to judgment. I deceive myself if I think I will go to heaven when I die, and I will get the shock of my life when my soul leaves my body at the point of death.

Satan wants us to believe that, as God created the whole human race, God will let the souls of the whole human race into heaven when we die. Sounds lovely doesn't it? But this is not the truth according to God's Word.

Yes, all are created in God's image (see Genesis 1:27), and God created the first human beings as perfect, but after Adam and Eve fell for Satan's deception in the Garden of Eden, the whole human race from that day onwards has been born with the inherent disposition of sin; and eternity in hell is the default position of all that is sinful and evil (see Revelation 21:27).

We personally cannot change this through our own efforts. We cannot get rid of this disposition ourselves; we need someone to save us from our sins (see Matthew 1:18-25, where the angel of the Lord declared to Joseph that Jesus would save His people (the Jews) from their sins; in Acts chapter 10, this salvation was then made available to all who become believers from the Gentile nations).

Like Adam and Eve, because of our inherent sin, God has banished us from His presence and from 'paradise'. The only way back for the whole human race is through the 'Door of Salvation' that God has opened, which is through faith in His Son, Jesus Christ (see John 10:1-17).

In our stubbornness and pride, we try to gain entry through a multitude of other 'doors' that do not involve having faith in Jesus, but none of these 'doors' will give us entry into God's heavenly Kingdom.

If 'all will be saved', regardless of our religious beliefs or none, then based on this thinking, God has sent His Son Jesus to us and He was crucified and shed His blood for **nothing**. This shows that Universalism is a lie from the pit of hell, as this kind of 'salvation' negates the Cross of Christ.

Universalism's teaching is designed to 'soothe us' with its lies that we don't need to repent of our sins, and that God is not a God of wrath or justice. People are getting sucked into this deception, including many followers of Christ, who want an 'easy walk' rather than the discipline of obedience to God's Holy Word. Universalism is deceiving millions of people who do not want to be convicted by the Holy Word of God that we are all sinners in God's sight, and in need of salvation through faith in the only Saviour, whom God sent to us. His name is Jesus Christ. He is the Messiah.

There is no other name by which we can be saved from eternity in hell.

"For Jesus is the one referred to in the Scriptures, where it says, 'The stone that you builders rejected has now become the cornerstone.' There is salvation in no one else! God has given no other name under heaven by which we must be saved." Acts 4:11-12 NLT

The false gospel of Universalism has been around for centuries, but it would seem that lately it has risen to new heights with the proliferation of books and movies that peddle this deception. I am stunned when I read articles that highlight the glaringly obvious apostasy of a growing number of Christian leaders who endorse such material, thereby causing their congregations to buy these books, or to flock to the latest 'blockbuster' movie version of such books.

Universalism is a snake from the pit of hell, which will entice you into its lair. When are followers of Christ going to start using the Word of God in order to discern the deception that is in front of their eyes when they read and watch these things, promoted under the label of 'Christianity'? It's time we woke up out of our slumber and repented of this apostasy, before it is too late!

Under this heading of Universalism, I will now write about the subject of 'religious dogma', which I mentioned in Chapter 1, as I feel that this subject may fit in better here than in any of the other sub-headings.

Religious Dogma

An online search will reveal that a basic definition of 'Dogma' is that it is a set of codes, beliefs and principles which are held to be necessarily true and cannot or will not change.

A very good article, which is helpful for followers of Christ to know when faced with the forceful opposition that can come our way when we steadfastly uphold the truth of God's Word, can be found on www.whatchristianswanttoknow.com, and is titled, "What is Christian Dogma? Should Christians Be Dogmatic?"

When I have been passionate about speaking the truth of the Word of God, I have experienced professing followers of Christ say that they don't want to be bound up with the 'restraints' of Church doctrine, which they sometimes vehemently refer to as 'religious dogma'.

Let's get this clear - The Word of God is Holy Scripture, inspired by the Creator of the universe; the Creator of all things! To resist and scoff at the Word of God, forcefully declaring Scripture and Church doctrine to be 'nothing but religious dogma' is to treat God's Word with contempt. People seem to aggressively express the term 'religious dogma' in a manner that implies that it is something that they must avoid at all costs.

Let us remind ourselves that Jesus Himself is the Word of God made flesh (see John 1:14), so when we state that God's Word (and hence Church doctrine) is just 'a load of religious dogma', which we could happily do without, we are in effect stating that Jesus (God's Word made flesh) is nothing but 'religious dogma' that we could do without!

Such people say that they believe in God and Jesus, but they want to be free to follow other kinds of spiritual teachings and practices too; ones which suit their disposition and make them feel comfortable and unchallenged, even if these teachings and practises are contrary to the authoritative Word of God, and are strictly forbidden in His Word.

They cite the Scriptures that say we are 'all children of God' because we are created in His image, and as such they claim that we don't need to be born-again. This denies what Jesus says in John chapter 3, where He said that unless we are born again, we cannot enter the Kingdom of Heaven.

They want to do away with what they call 'religious dogma', when in reality what they want to do away with is Biblical doctrine and teachings which they find uncomfortable, and replace it with something more 'convenient' to their preferences.

Sadly, many churches today are abandoning the Spiritual security of religious dogma, and are joining in with this kind of thinking. In order to attract people to their church, they are re-shaping their services and practices, and are preaching and teaching whatever the next cultural 'trend' is. Knowingly, or unknowingly, the Church of today has bitten the forbidden fruit, and is embracing and teaching 'new expressions of Christianity', many of which are things that God's Word has warned and commanded us **not** to do.

It is the Garden of Eden all over again. Where obedience to the Word of God is concerned, Satan is subtly whispering into the ears of church leaders on every level, saying, " Did God really say that? Is that what God really meant?" And so church leaders begin to question and doubt the truth of God's Word; the uncompromising truth that their church ancestors have firmly believed and obeyed for decades and even centuries before them.

Bit by bit, the Church is forsaking God's Word and replacing Scriptures and doctrine with teachings of the secular world which they consider to be more 'palatable'; teachings which they deem to be more 'loving' and 'embracing', which they want to use to replace the Holy Scriptures that they find too challenging to accept any more, let alone obey.

The Bible states that Jesus is the same yesterday, today and forever (see Hebrews 13:8). As Jesus is the Word of God made flesh, it goes without saying that God's Word (the Holy Bible) is also the same yesterday, today and forever. So, when we mess about with God's Word and the vital, godly, grounding dogma of the Church, ripping big chunks out and inserting our own replacement 'word', yet still label our replacements with the hallowed title of 'Holy Scripture', and still call ourselves 'followers of Christ', and still call our church a 'Christian' church, we must surely be in the deepest of deception.

True Christianity is the uncompromising, unwavering, challenging preaching and teaching of the Word of God, which brings conviction of sin, godly sorrow, confession and repentance, which then leads to salvation. When people in the Bible did not like what Jesus taught them, He did not 'back-peddle' and try to soften His teachings. No, He let the people struggle with His teachings, even to the point that many of them walked away from Him and followed Him no more (see John 6:66). Jesus did not run after them and try to appease them or apologise for any hurt that His teachings may have caused them. He did not do an 'about-turn' and say that He did not mean what He said. He simply let His Word penetrate to the core of their souls, and let them walk away.

This is what the Church is meant to do. We are meant to preach God's Word as it is, and then let it do its convicting work in the souls of those we preach to. We are supposed to do what Jesus did, and let the people walk away if they don't like His teachings.

On these issues, Chambers says,

"If a person cannot go to God, it is because he has something secret which he does not intend to give up – he may admit his sin, but would no more give up that thing than he could fly under his own power. It is impossible to deal sympathetically with people like that. We must reach down deep in their lives to the root of the problem, which will cause hostility and resentment toward the message. People want the blessing of God, but they can't stand something that pierces right through to the heart of the matter.

If you are sensitive to God's way, your message as His servant will be merciless and insistent, cutting to the very root. Otherwise, there will be no healing. We must drive the message home so forcefully that a person cannot possibly hide, but must apply its truth. Deal with people where they are, until they begin to realise their true need. Then hold high the standard of Jesus for their lives." (Excerpt from December 19th) [1]

Again, Chambers says,

"...if a New Testament standard is revealed to us by the light of God, and we don't try to measure up, or even feel inclined to do so, then we begin to backslide. It means your conscience does not respond to the truth. You can never be the same after the unveiling of a truth. That moment marks you out as one who either continues on with even more devotion as a disciple of Jesus Christ, or as one who turns to go back as a deserter." (Excerpt from December 29th) [2]

The trouble is that the Church seems to now be afraid of preaching the truth of God's Word in case it hurts, upsets or even offends people; the Gospel message which once brought people to their knees under the convicting power of the Holy Spirit, bringing confession and repentance upon them, enabling them to turn to Jesus to save them.

The Church is now increasingly succumbing to the demands of the 'politically correct' approach of making everyone feel comfortable and happy, preferring to please man rather than God, where conviction, confession and repentance is either 'optional', or worst still, no longer necessary.

The consequence of this is that those who are caught up in this Spiritual vs natural tug-of-war, don't know what to do with the centuries of sound, godly teachings and doctrines that have held the Church together against the opposing forces of darkness since the day the Church was born (in Act chapter 2). Rather than repent and obey God's Word, they begin to convince themselves that God's tough teachings, which make people feel uncomfortable, are no longer relevant for the twenty-first century.

I have to say this; I really do not know how church leaders who are throwing away established and sound Church dogma for the sake of people's comfort, sleep at night. They are supposed to be looking out for our souls, not leading us onto the highway to hell (see Chapter 5 – Which Path Are You On?).

Praying to and worshipping angels, Mary, the apostles and saints of old, and any other idols.

The Bible says that angels are messengers who are sent to minister to those who will inherit salvation (see Hebrews 1:14).

That is awesome! My daughter and I have had the humbling experience of being blessed by several visible angelic interventions and protection in times of need, so although I haven't got room in this book to give these testimonies, I know that angelic assistance is very real!

However, a word of caution: we are **not** supposed to directly ask angels to help us. We must call out to **God** to help us, and if He so chooses, He will dispatch His angels to help us. If He does so, and we are actually privileged to be aware of such an encounter with a ministering angel, we must be sure to give the glory and thanks to God, not to the angels. Angels are just carrying out the will of God, and they do not need or want our thanks for it.

Do not fall into the trap of 'praying to or calling on the angels' to help you, because this is contrary to the Word of God, as it will cause you to place your trust and faith in them rather than God. Calling on the angels and worshipping angels is the teaching and practice of some alternative 'spiritual' organisations, and it is not the will of God.

Praying to or calling on the angels for help and guidance can open us up to being visited and assisted by Satan himself, and his demons, who are more than happy to deceive people by 'masquerading as angels of light' (see 2 Corinthians 11:14-15).

This is why the Word of God warns us to worship only God because He knows what will happen if we project our focus and our prayers on to other spiritual beings. It will cause us to be led into deception because we will believe we have had holy angelic assistance or guidance, but will not realise that it was in fact Satan or his demons masquerading as angels of light. Satan will use any opportunity to gain entrance into our lives, and it only takes a tiny amount of our deviating from the truth of God's Word for Satan to succeed in his evil plans of deception.

In the Book of Revelation, an angel appeared to the apostle John, and John fell at the angel's feet as though dead. But the angel rebuked John and told him to stand up on his feet and told him not to worship him, as he was just a servant like John was, and that John was to worship only God. This happened on two separate occasions (see Revelation 19:10; 22:8-9)!

So be sure to pray to God and to worship God only, and do not get caught in the trap of praying to any of God's created beings, not even Mary (the Mother of Jesus) or any of the apostles. If the holy angelic host do not want us to pray to or worship angels, how much more would the apostles and Mary herself not want us to do this in relation to themselves! They would be exhorting us to worship God and His Son Jesus Christ. Mary did not die on the Cross for our sins, nor did any of the apostles. Our prayers and our worship should therefore be to God the Father, and His Son Jesus Christ.

Having said this, I am aware that many believers do pray to angels, to Mary and the saints of old who are now dead, and kneel before statues of them in their Church buildings. With the deepest of love for all who do this with sincerity of heart, I feel that I must set before you what God's Word has to say about these kinds of religious practices, and then exhort you to repent.

"The idols of the nations are merely things of silver and gold, shaped by human hands. They have mouths but cannot speak, and eyes but cannot see. They have ears but cannot hear, and noses but cannot smell. And those who make idols are just like them, as are all who trust in them." Psalm 135:15-18 NLT

"What fools they are who carry around their wooden idols and pray to gods that cannot save!" Isaiah 45:20(b) NLT

"What good is an idol carved by man,
  or a cast image that deceives you?
How foolish to trust in your own creation —
  a god that can't even talk!
What sorrow awaits you who say to wooden idols,
  'Wake up and save us!'
To speechless stone images you say,
  'Rise up and teach us!'
 Can an idol tell you what to do?
They may be overlaid with gold and silver,
  but they are lifeless inside.
But the LORD is in his holy Temple.
Let all the earth be silent before him."
Habakkuk 2:18-20 NLT

"But the people...still refused to repent of their evil deeds and turn to God. They continued to worship demons and idols made of

gold, silver, bronze, stone and wood – idols that can neither see, nor hear, nor walk!" Revelation 9:20 NLT

God's Word is very stern about engaging in this kind of activity. He does not want us to do this. It can open us up to being deceived by Satan and his demons masquerading as angels of light, which is why we should obey the Word of God and **only** pray to God and worship **only** Him; God, being the Father, Son and the Holy Spirit.

Alternative 'spirituality'

The world is awash with a multitude of things claiming to be 'spiritual', flooding the market to entice all who are seeking 'enlightenment'. Instead of turning to Jesus in confession and repentance of our sins and receiving forgiveness and the assurance of salvation and eternal life in heaven, we are trying to comfort ourselves, and heal and save our own soul by turning to this multitude of counterfeits:

Satanism, Witchcraft and the Occult; consulting mediums, clairvoyants and contacting the spirits of the dead; dowsing, divining, crystals, orbs, Ouija boards and séances.

Ghost-hunting; hypnosis and hypnotherapy or anything involving 'mind-control'; palm reading, tea-leaf reading, fortune-telling, tarot cards, horoscopes, astrology, yoga, levitation, and channelling.

New Age and other alternative spiritualism; Eastern mystic spiritualism, chanting and mystical-style 'worship', and anything associated with it;

Alternative spiritual 'healing' groups where faith in God/ Jesus Christ is absent from their beliefs; a multitude of other 'healing' practises that are commonly known as 'alternative or complimentary medicine', many of which have their origins in paganism. Labyrinths; Lectio Divina.

Scientology; Freemasonry and affiliated Organisations; any

'faith' or religion that denies God and/or His Son Jesus Christ as the Messiah and our Lord and Saviour; cults and sects, even so-called 'Christian' cults.

This list is not exhaustive; there are many more.

I exhort you to avoid these things, and any practice that is not rooted in God and His Son Jesus Christ. All counterfeits will subtly lead you astray and into Satan's grip, from which you will then need deliverance. This experience is a gruelling process, and Satan and his demons will 'kick up a stink' when you try to get yourself free. So don't get involved in these counterfeits in the first place.

Emerging Church 'Christianity'

There are many high-profile leaders who are throwing off the mantle of almost 2000 years of 'doing Church'. They have had enough of it, and want to 'do Church' differently. This shift is the rise of the 'Emerging Church' of today. Many of these leaders have websites and have written books, and their message is drawing people away from the authentic Christianity of two millennia.

I once read a statement that said, "Love is the absence of Judgment". This sounds lovely and soothing to our weary souls, doesn't it?

But as we are seeing already in this book, God's Word written in the Holy Bible is saying that the **rejection** of **God's love**, given to us in His Son Jesus Christ, **will** bring judgment. This is God's truth. The statement that "Love is the absence of Judgment" is a lie from Satan, designed to deceptively 'comfort' us.

The Emerging Church is a movement, involving many aspects of life today, with a desire to reach people with the gentle witness of God's love, rather than the powerful convicting witness of the Holy Spirit, which would bring people to repentance. This sounds okay on the face of it, but forsaking almost 2000 years of Christianity that has gone before is not a wise thing to do. Such action is saying to God that all that has gone before is a mistake and a failure. It's as if we want to 'play God', deciding that we think we know what is the right way to 'do Church' from now on, because the 'old ways' aren't working. Who are we to decide what is working and what isn't? I thought that was God's role? The Church today seems to be obsessed with the external visibility of results and success as their 'guide' to whether things are working.

Much of the modern Church wants 'bums on seats' at the expense of obedience to Biblical truth. It is prepared to embrace, accept and do anything in order to bring people in, and look good in the eyes of the world, and thereby increase its reputation and its standing in the wider community.

An example of this is the current movement called 'Spiritual Formation', which is sweeping across many Christian denominations, with its appeal to adults who feel disillusioned with the state of the Church, and also to the younger generation who may have no interest in or even a dislike for the established Church. Many high-profile church leaders are being hoodwinked by the subtle deception of this movement, and are feeding it to their congregations.

Briefly, the focus of 'Spiritual Formation' is on emptying our minds and our hearts of everything so that we can 'hear from God'. This is in stark contrast to the many Scriptures in God's Word, which teach us to read His Word, feed upon it, and meditate on it so that we are **transformed** by the renewing of our minds (see Romans 12:2).

We must let the truth of God's Word penetrate our minds and our hearts, and transform us into right living, **not** empty our minds and expose ourselves to hearing nice-sounding words in our minds that are the 'teachings' of demons masquerading as angels of light. If what we hear in our empty minds are words that are contrary to God's Word, then we can be sure that what we have heard is **not** from God.

Beloved in Christ, I urge you to repent and flee from such deception and return to sound and wholesome teaching from God's Word. As followers of Christ, we only need His teachings to guide us, help us and change us. We do not need the nice-sounding but ultimately deceptive teachings of those whose desire is to ensnare us and lead us astray. Research this movement for yourself and expose the light of Christ onto what its 'teachings' are. Then escape from its web of lies and turn back to the truth of the Word of God… nothing else.

I listened to a powerful radio interview with Pastor Gary Gilley on www.standforthetruth.com, who was talking to the interviewer about the 'Spiritual Formation' movement. I would encourage anyone who is involved in this movement to listen to this interview. Your eyes will be opened so that you can see the 'way of escape'.

Much of the Emerging Church is embracing all kinds of teaching and practices from other 'spiritual' beliefs, many of these having Eastern or Pagan origins, and people are soaking this up like sponges. Because all these things sound new and nice, and even appear 'Spiritual', like a 'new path' that God has revealed to them, church leaders and their flock are rushing ahead and implementing these things instead of 'testing the spirits' (see 1 John 4:1), which God's Word exhorts us to do.

But the Lord warns us, in the following proverb, of the consequences of following ways which we think are right, but in fact will end in disaster.

"There is a way that seems right to a man and appears straight before him, but at the end of it is the way of death." Proverbs 16:25 AMPC

Aside from the above example of 'Spiritual Formation', this section does not intend to go into detail of what the 'gospel' of the Emerging Church is or what it looks like, but will list below some other examples of what is currently out there, so that you can do the research for yourself.

Examples of the 'Emerging Church'

a) Lukewarm Christianity

Many 'Emerging' churches are now preaching a watered-down alternative 'Word of God' (another 'gospel'), making it more palatable for newcomers, as well as less challenging to existing believers; no longer telling people what they must do to be saved (see Acts chapter 2); refraining from preaching about being born-again (which is contrary to what Jesus said in John chapter 3); omitting to preach about being baptised by full immersion (see Matthew chapter 3), and being filled with the Holy Spirit (see Acts chapter 2); no longer warning or exhorting the flock to keep watchful, alert, and ready for the Lord's return (see Matthew 24 & Mark 13); failing to preach and teach about the reality of hell (see the Scriptures I have put in chapter 5).

Some churches are preaching a 'gospel' of 'Christianity without the Cross' (see Matthew chapter 27, Mark chapter 15, Luke Chapter 23 & John chapter 19 for the evidence of Jesus being crucified on the Cross).

Others are preaching that God didn't really create the world, and prefer to go along with the theory of Evolution (see Genesis Chapter 1 for the evidence that God created everything).

There are leaders who claim there was never a virgin birth (see Matthew 1:18-25, for the angelic declaration that Mary was a virgin). Some churches feel they have no need to conduct the service of the Lord's Supper (Holy Communion), whilst others only take a part of it, and still others conduct it in a rather casual and almost irreverent manner (see what the apostle Paul has to say about this in 1 Corinthians 11:23-32).

All these things are the foundations of the Christian faith, so if they are no longer preaching these things, what exactly is it that they do at their church services?!

On the matter of 'Christianity without the Cross', Chambers says this:

"All the pleading for salvation which deliberately ignores the Cross of Christ is useless. It is knocking at a door other than the one which Jesus has already opened. We protest by saying, "But I don't want to come in that way. It is too humiliating to be received as a sinner." God's response, through Peter is, "…there is no other name…by which we must be saved" (Acts 4:12)." (Excerpt from December 8th) [4]

The Spiritual Gifts

Along with the above, there are churches that teach that the gifts of the Holy Spirit, such as the gift of tongues, interpretation and prophecy, healing, and casting out demons, are 'no longer for today'. Some even say that these gifts are 'of the devil'.

Let's get this straight. How can the Spiritual gifts – given to the Church by God, to be used for His glory, so freely used in the early Church, and written down in Holy Scripture for us all to see – now suddenly be of the devil, simply because the people who are saying this believe that the Spiritual gifts ceased once those early believers died?

To state that the Spiritual gifts are now 'of the devil' must surely be bordering on blasphemy against the Holy Spirit, or at the very least this must grieve the Holy Spirit deeply. Can we not see Satan's deception in this? Open your eyes, Church! Wake up!

Such teaching is contrary to the Word of God because Jesus Himself said that 'signs will follow' those who **believe**. They will cast out demons, and will speak with new tongues (see Mark 16:17). Whilst much of the Church is in a serious state of apostasy and unbelief concerning the Spiritual gifts, there are still a great many faithful believers who are filled with the Holy Spirit, and are displaying these gifts in abundance. Praise God!

The Need for Regular Repentance

Many churches preach that we don't need to keep confessing and repenting of our daily sins – in effect they are saying that if we sin, just forget about it and get on with life, because God loves us and forgives us, so our sin doesn't matter anymore. They preach that it is okay for us to remain the way we are, with obedience to God's Word now being relegated to the category of 'optional'. It's a preaching that says. "You repented once at the start, when you gave your life to Christ, so that covers you for everything, so when you sin, don't worry about it."

This is contrary to what Jesus spoke to the woman caught in the act of adultery, when He said to her, "Go now, and leave your life of sin" (see John 8:11).

In the King James Version it says, "Go, and sin no more."

Jesus' command to "Go, and sin no more" is as loud as a trumpet blast! But Satan has deceived much of the Church, causing us to believe that whilst there is forgiveness for our sins, we can still carry on doing the very things that Jesus commanded us to repent of.

Many churches are failing to preach that we must crucify our flesh (see Galatians 5:24) and that we must sin **no more** (see John 8:11). This latter Scripture is a **command** of Jesus, not an optional extra!

Speaking to followers of Christ concerning how we should live until the day we see Jesus, the apostle John says,

"Dear friends, we are already God's children, but he has not yet shown us what we will be like when Christ appears. But we do know that we will be like him, for we will see him as he really is. And all who have this eager expectation will keep themselves pure, just as he is pure.

Everyone who sins is breaking God's law, for all sin is contrary

to the law of God. And you know that Jesus came to take away our sins, and there is no sin in him. Anyone who continues to live in him will not sin. But anyone who keeps on sinning does not know him or understand who he is.

Dear children, don't let anyone deceive you about this: When people do what is right, it shows that they are righteous, even as Christ is righteous. But when people keep on sinning, it shows that they belong to the devil, who has been sinning since the beginning. But the Son of God came to destroy the works of the devil. Those who have been born into God's family do not make a practice of sinning, because God's life is in them. So they can't keep on sinning, because they are children of God." 1 John 3:2-9 NLT

Silence Condones Sin

A last word on 'Lukewarm Christianity'; many church leaders are silent on a whole host of matters that God's Word has a lot to say about. To remain silent about God's Word, when sin is running rampant in our churches, is to condone sin. Unless leaders repent and clean up God's House, God will hold His leaders accountable. Read how God feels about His shepherds, who neglect their flock, in the Old Testament passage below.

"Therefore, you shepherds, hear the word of the LORD: As surely as I live, says the Sovereign LORD, you abandoned my flock and left them to be attacked by every wild animal. And though you were my shepherds, you didn't search for my sheep when they were lost. You took care of yourselves and left the sheep to starve. Therefore, you shepherds, hear the word of the LORD. This is what the Sovereign LORD says: I now consider these shepherds my enemies, and I will hold them responsible for what has happened to my flock. I will take away their right to feed the flock, and I will stop them from feeding themselves. I will rescue my flock from their mouths; the sheep will no longer be their prey." Ezekiel 34:7-10 NLT

b) 'Wolves in sheep's clothing'

Briefly, these are leaders in the Church, who Jesus refers to as 'wolves in sheep's clothing' and 'hired hands' (see John 10:6-13), who are not really interested or concerned for the flock, but are in the business of leading churches for the money (see 2 Corinthians 2:17), the prestige, and the perks of the job which may include free housing. I have encountered this in my years as a follower of Christ.

To illustrate this, below is the powerful parable of the weeds and the wheat. Jesus is referring to the 'enemy' planting weeds amongst the fields of wheat. We can take this as a direct message for today's lukewarm, complacent and compromising Church and its leaders.

In this parable, we can interpret the 'enemy' as being Satan, the 'weeds' as being Satan's counterfeit church leaders, the 'wheat' referring to the faithful and obedient followers of Christ and faithful church leaders, and the 'fields (of wheat)' as being the faithful Church.

It is clear in this passage that the enemy's weeds will remain amongst the fields of wheat right up until the final harvest. The Lord will then separate the evil weeds from the good wheat, and will burn the weeds (in the furnace of fire – Matthew 13:40-42 KJV). The wheat He will gather into His barn (Kingdom of Heaven).

Here is the parable:

"Here is another story Jesus told: "The Kingdom of Heaven is like a farmer who planted good seed in his field. But that night as the workers slept, his enemy came and planted weeds among the wheat, then slipped away. When the crop began to grow and produce grain, the weeds also grew.

"The farmer's workers went to him and said, 'Sir, the field where you planted that good seed is full of weeds! Where did they come from?'

"'An enemy has done this!' the farmer exclaimed.

"'Should we pull out the weeds?' they asked.

"'No,' he replied, 'you'll uproot the wheat if you do. Let both grow together until the harvest. Then I will tell the harvesters to sort out the weeds, tie them into bundles, and burn them, and to put the wheat in the barn.'" Matthew 13: 24-30 NLT

Church leaders; when we read this parable, does its serious warnings not cause us any concern about the way we are leading our churches, and the eternal destiny of ourselves and our flock? Wake up!

c) Replacement Theology and Rising Anti-Semitism in the Christian Church

Again, it is not the intention of this book to enter into any deep discussion on the subject of this heading. I am simply going to show a couple of passages from God's Word concerning His beloved nation Israel, and her precious people.

Whilst this subject is an issue that has been a part of the Christian Church for a very long time, I felt the need to mention it under this section of 'Emerging Christianity'.

Over the past few decades, the Church seems to have failed to teach believers about the history of the Jews, and how it came about that Salvation was made available to the Gentile nations. I say this from experience, as one who spent three-quarters of my life to date as a follower of Christ but with absolutely no interest in Church history, until 2011, when God started to reveal things to me, which caused the veil to drop from my eyes regarding Israel.

With many in today's Church not having much interest in or knowledge concerning the Jewish roots of Christianity, over the past few years particularly there seems to have been a resurgence of Anti-Semitic thinking within the 'Emerging' Church of our times.

As professing followers of Christ, let us first remind ourselves that, in the Bible, God is known as the 'God of Israel' (see Exodus 5:1, Matthew 15:3, & Luke 1:68). Let us also remind ourselves that God's Son, Jesus Christ (known as Yeshua HaMashiach to Jews who have received Him as their Saviour), was a Jew and raised in a Jewish household, observing all of the Jewish customs (see Luke chapter 2), and teaching in the synagogues. We also know from Scripture that His first disciples were all Jewish, as He referred to them as 'brothers' (for example, see Matthew chapter 4). It would not have been the custom in those times to refer to people of Gentile nations as 'brothers'.

With this basic knowledge, and with the Scripture passages below, we will clearly see that Replacement Theology is a 'false gospel', one of Satan's most evil counterfeits, which is raising its ugly head in the Christian Church, deceiving many into believing that God has abandoned and forsaken the Children of Israel because of their rejection of His Son, Jesus Christ, Yeshua HaMashiach.

God has **not** 'replaced' Israel with the Gentile followers of Christ in the Christian Church! In God's mercy for the Gentile believers, He has 'grafted us in' to His plan of Salvation. To 'graft something in', means that the original 'stock' is still there, as the main root. The 'grafted in' part is just a branch attached to the main rootstock. God has not dug up His beloved Israel and slung her onto the trash heap! His love and mercy for her remains the same as it did at the beginning, and He will not forsake her.

For the Christian Church to believe the Anti-Semitic doctrine of Replacement Theology, and to begin expressing it in agreeing with the application of BDS (Boycott, Divestment and Sanctions) against Israel, is to actually enter into what most of the world is now doing to Israel on an escalating basis. The world, and much of the Church, is cursing Israel, and God has got something to say about it, as we will now see.

Speaking to Abraham, God said,

"I will make you into a great nation. I will bless you and make you famous, and you will be a blessing to others. I will bless those who bless you and curse those who treat you with contempt. All the families on earth will be blessed through you." Genesis 12:2-3 NLT

God is saying that He will curse those who curse Israel. This is not just a warning to the nations of the world who currently curse Israel with BDS, and some nations even expressing a desire to wipe Israel off the map; it is a warning to followers of Christ in the Christian Church who get involved in any practice that directly or indirectly curses or harms Israel. We must fall on our faces in repentance immediately, or face the consequences, as individuals, corporately as the Church, and also as nations.

God is watching.

Let's look at what the apostle Paul wrote to the believers in Rome, on the matter of God's chosen people, Israel. We will see that, right from the start, the early Church was being deceived with this insidious doctrine of 'Replacement Theology'. But what excuse does the Church today have in keeping this lie alive, when we have God-inspired Holy Scripture such as what we are about to read, to rebuke us and correct our thinking?

It is a long passage, but I exhort you to read the whole thing, because only then will we be able to escape from Satan's lie about Israel, when we come to the knowledge of the truth from God's Word.

God's Mercy on Israel

"I ask, then, has God rejected his own people, the nation of Israel? Of course not! I myself am an Israelite, a descendant of Abraham and a member of the tribe of Benjamin.

No, God has not rejected his own people, whom he chose from the very beginning. Do you realize what the Scriptures say about this? Elijah the prophet complained to God about the people of Israel and

said, "LORD, they have killed your prophets and torn down your altars. I am the only one left, and now they are trying to kill me, too."

And do you remember God's reply? He said, "No, I have 7,000 others who have never bowed down to Baal!"

It is the same today, for a few of the people of Israel have remained faithful because of God's grace — his undeserved kindness in choosing them. And since it is through God's kindness, then it is not by their good works. For in that case, God's grace would not be what it really is — free and undeserved.

So this is the situation: Most of the people of Israel have not found the favor of God they are looking for so earnestly. A few have — the ones God has chosen — but the hearts of the rest were hardened. As the Scriptures say,

"God has put them into a deep sleep.

To this day he has shut their eyes so they do not see, and closed their ears so they do not hear."

Likewise, David said,

"Let their bountiful table become a snare,
  a trap that makes them think all is well.
Let their blessings cause them to stumble,
  and let them get what they deserve.

Let their eyes go blind so they cannot see, and let their backs be bent forever."

Did God's people stumble and fall beyond recovery? Of course not! They were disobedient, so God made salvation available to the Gentiles. But he wanted his own people to become jealous and claim it for themselves. Now if the Gentiles were enriched because the people of Israel turned down God's offer of salvation, think how much greater a blessing the world will share when they finally accept it.

I am saying all this especially for you Gentiles. God has appointed me as the apostle to the Gentiles. I stress this, for I want somehow *to make the people of Israel jealous of what you Gentiles have, so I might save some of them. For since their rejection meant that God offered salvation to the rest of the world, their acceptance will be even more wonderful. It will be life for those who were dead! And since Abraham and the other patriarchs were holy, their descendants will also be holy — just as the entire batch of dough is holy because the portion given as an offering is holy. For if the roots of the tree are holy, the branches will be, too.*

But some of these branches from Abraham's tree — some of the people of Israel — have been broken off. And you Gentiles, who were branches from a wild olive tree, have been grafted in. So now you also receive the blessing God has promised Abraham and his children, sharing in the rich nourishment from the root of God's special olive tree. But you must not brag about being grafted in to replace the branches that were broken off. You are just a branch, not the root.

"Well," you may say, "those branches were broken off to make room for me." Yes, but remember — those branches were broken off because they didn't believe in Christ, and you are there because you do believe. So don't think highly of yourself, but fear what could happen. For if God did not spare the original branches, he won't spare you either.

Notice how God is both kind and severe. He is severe toward those who disobeyed, but kind to you if you continue to trust in his kindness. But if you stop trusting, you also will be cut off. And if the people of Israel turn from their unbelief, they will be grafted in again, for God has the power to graft them back into the tree. You, by nature, were a branch cut from a wild olive tree. So if God was willing to do something contrary to nature by grafting you into his cultivated tree, he will be far more eager to graft the original branches back into the tree where they belong.

I want you to understand this mystery, dear brothers and sisters, so that you will not feel proud about yourselves. Some of the people of Israel have hard hearts, but this will last only until the full number of Gentiles comes to Christ. And so all Israel will be saved. As the

Scriptures say,

"The one who rescues will come from Jerusalem,
and he will turn Israel away from ungodliness.
And this is my covenant with them,
that I will take away their sins."

Many of the people of Israel are now enemies of the Good News,
and this benefits you Gentiles. Yet they are still the people he loves
because he chose their ancestors Abraham, Isaac, and Jacob. For God's
gifts and his call can never be withdrawn." Romans 11:1-29 NLT

This is the Word of the Lord, and I will leave it do its convicting work in the hearts of those in the Church, whose eyes have been veiled to this truth.

d) The 'Silent', Social gospel

The ethos of this is, "Let's do the work and meet the needs, but we won't preach about Jesus. We will just 'be Jesus' to the people, so that they can see God's love."

This is contrary to God's Word, because the apostle Paul says, concerning people who have not heard about Jesus Christ,

"But how can they call on him to save them unless they believe in
him? And how can they believe in him if they have never heard about
him? And how can they hear about him unless someone tells them?
And how will anyone go and tell them without being sent? That is
why the Scriptures say, "How beautiful are the feet of messengers who
bring good news!" Romans 10:13-15 NLT

Clearly we are meant to speak about Jesus, not just do 'good works' in our communities and the wider world.

Many churches have opened their doors as a 'marketplace' in order to raise funds for the church building, or for their projects. More people seem to come to the church buildings to get involved in whatever the church may be hosting, rather than to hear the

Gospel; events such as flower festivals, craft fairs, Christmas tree festivals, May Day festivals, and social and community activities (some of which ought never to be occurring in the House of God, because of their Pagan origins).

Many of the activities we allow to take place in our church buildings are spiritually desecrating the House of God. This reminds me of when Jesus entered the Temple and saw people 'doing business'. He became really angry, - with a righteous anger - that people had turned the House of God into a 'den of thieves' (see Matthew 21:12-14).

But when we allow other people to use our church building, are we sharing the Gospel with these people when they come in, or are we just letting them use the House of God for their community activities? It would seem that church leaders would prefer to be seen to be reaching out to the community to 'please man' by meeting the social needs, rather than please God by reaching out to the community with the Gospel message of forgiveness of sins and salvation through faith in Jesus Christ. People's souls will not be saved from hell just because we may be a 'nice minister' who lets the community use the House of God for their activities.

Yes, we do need to do these good works, but not to the exclusion of preaching the Gospel message. We need to deliver the message and do the deeds. When we run a soup kitchen for the homeless and those in poverty, we need to give them the 'Bread of Life' to save their souls from eternity in hell, as well as give them actual bread to save them from starvation.

e) The Prosperity 'gospel'

This false gospel is rampant in today's church culture, with its message of "send us your 'best gift' and God will bless you and give you wealth, healing, and breakthrough." This is subtle manipulation, preying on desperate people, and it lines the pockets and the lifestyles of those who are peddling this deception, building their own 'kingdoms' of wealth and affluence, instead of the Kingdom of God (see 2 Corinthians 2:17).

Primarily it is God's will that we prosper spiritually. However, there are Scriptures that say that we will reap what we sow in this life (see Mark 10:29-30), which suggests that we may also prosper in a material and financial sense, but the kind of manipulation mentioned in the previous paragraph is not the way to go about receiving God's provision. In fact, Jesus teaches that we should sell all we have and give it to the poor (see Matthew 19:21-22). This is in stark contrast to the affluent lifestyles of some of our high-profile 'celebrity' Christian leaders.

If God does prosper us abundantly, both materially and financially, that is a wonderful blessing, but we are not to horde it to ourselves and have a proud attitude that says, "Look at me! Look at all that I have got! God must think I am really great to give me all this prosperity and success!"

When we are blessed with God's abundance, we are exhorted to sow it back into God's Kingdom by giving to those who are struggling and oppressed, helping the poor, the widows and the orphans. Society is awash with the evidence of poverty and injustice, so there are plenty of things that we can sow our abundance into for God's glory.

Do not bow down to the kind of 'Christianity' which majors on promoting and preaching the 'prosperity gospel'. Check your Bible to see whether or not what they are teaching lines up with Scripture. If it doesn't, obey what Jesus tells you to do, not what these false teachers subtly manipulate you to do.

f) Unrepentant sexual immorality (all types) and homosexuality *within* the Church; homosexual 'marriage', and homosexual Church leaders.

There is an abundance of discussions and debates on this subject in both the Church and secular arenas, and so I do not intend to discuss this subject in detail. But I will start by saying that, through Jesus' sacrifice on the Cross, God's grace, mercy, and forgiveness for our sins has been made available for the whole human race, whatever our sins may be. We can receive His loving gifts to us this very day through confession and repentance of our sins, and following Christ by obeying His Word.

But there is a Day coming when this period of grace, mercy and forgiveness will cease. The 'Day' I am referring to is known in the Bible as the Day of Judgment. God does not want anyone to perish but for all to come to repentance (see 2 Peter 3:9) before that fearful Day arrives, because that is the point when His grace, mercy and forgiveness will cease. Those who have given their lives to Christ and have repented of their sins will spend eternity in Heaven; but those who have not will spend eternity with Satan in Hell.

The purpose of this book is to expose Satan's counterfeits so that church leaders and their flock can come to their senses (see Luke Chapter 15), and then confront Satan's lies with God's Word in the same way that Jesus did when Satan was twisting the Word of God in his attempt to 'persuade' Jesus to obey and worship him. What was Jesus' response to Satan's deceptions?

Jesus said, **"It is written..."** (see Matthew 4:4,6,7,10 & Luke 4:4,8,10).

With all kinds of sexual immorality now being either openly regarded as acceptable in the Church, or being indulged in secretly behind our closed doors, or 'hidden' on computers in our homes, it is time that we purposefully remove the veil that has been covering our eyes, and put aside every belief or opinion we hold concerning this subject, especially where our thinking is contrary to God's Word.

Fornication, adultery, masturbation, pornography, homosexuality and other variations of sexuality, are running rampant in the Church, and it seems that very few are prepared to confront and deal with it. Recently, available to read on the Internet is the issue of transgender pastors, stating openly that 'God is transgender'. All these behaviours are so far from the truth of God's Holy Word that we can only deal with them by revealing what His Word says, for all of us to see.

So, let us **indeed** read what is written, at length. As hard as this may be to accept, what God's Word says is written out of His heart of love for us, and for our eternal destiny, for our salvation is at stake if we continue to reject His Word and remain in our rebellion.

Here is the Word of the Lord

"So God created man in His own image; in the image of God He created him; male and female He created them." Genesis 1:27 NKJV

"Then the LORD God said, "It is not good for the man to be alone. I will make a helper who is just right for him." So the LORD God formed from the ground all the wild animals and all the birds of the sky. He brought them to the man to see what he would call them, and the man chose a name for each one. He gave names to all the livestock, all the birds of the sky, and all the wild animals. But still there was no helper just right for him. So the LORD God caused the man to fall into a deep sleep. While the man slept, the LORD God took out one of the man's ribs and closed up the opening. Then the LORD God made a woman from the rib, and he brought her to the man.

"At last!" the man exclaimed.

"This one is bone from my bone,
and flesh from my flesh!
She will be called 'woman,'
because she was taken from 'man.'"

This explains why a man leaves his father and mother and is joined to his wife, and the two are united into one." Genesis 2:18-24 NLT

"Do not practice homosexuality, having sex with another man as

with a woman. It is a detestable sin." Leviticus 18:22 NLT

"If a man practices homosexuality, having sex with another man as with a woman, both men have committed a detestable act. They must both be put to death, for they are guilty of a capital offense." Leviticus 20:13 NLT

"Don't you realize that those who do wrong will not inherit the Kingdom of God? Don't fool yourselves. Those who indulge in sexual sin, or who worship idols, or commit adultery, or are male prostitutes, or practice homosexuality, or are thieves, or greedy people, or drunkards, or are abusive, or cheat people — none of these will inherit the Kingdom of God." 1 Corinthians 6: 9-10 NLT

"For the law was not intended for people who do what is right. It is for people who are lawless and rebellious, who are ungodly and sinful, who consider nothing sacred and defile what is holy, who kill their father or mother or commit other murders. The law is for people who are sexually immoral, or who practice homosexuality, or are slave traders, liars, promise breakers, or who do anything else that contradicts the wholesome teaching that comes from the glorious Good News entrusted to me by our blessed God." 1 Timothy 1:9 -11 NLT

"But God shows his anger from heaven against all sinful, wicked people who suppress the truth by their wickedness. They know the truth about God because he has made it obvious to them. For ever since the world was created, people have seen the earth and sky. Through everything God made, they can clearly see his invisible qualities — his eternal power and divine nature. So they have no excuse for not knowing God.

Yes, they knew God, but they wouldn't worship him as God or even give him thanks. And they began to think up foolish ideas of what God was like. As a result, their minds became dark and confused. Claiming to be wise, they instead became utter fools. And instead of worshiping the glorious, ever-living God, they worshiped idols made to look like mere people and birds and animals and reptiles.

So God abandoned them to do whatever shameful things their hearts desired. As a result, they did vile and degrading things with each other's bodies. They traded the truth about God for a lie. So they worshiped and served the things God created instead of the Creator himself, who is worthy of eternal praise! Amen. That is why God abandoned them to their shameful desires. Even the women turned against the natural way to have sex and instead indulged in sex with each other. And the men, instead of having normal sexual relations with women, burned with lust for each other. Men did shameful things with other men, and as a result of this sin, they suffered within themselves the penalty they deserved." Romans 1:18-27 NLT

"I can hardly believe the report about the sexual immorality going on among you — something that even pagans don't do." 1 Corinthians 5:1 NLT

"You say, "I am allowed to do anything" — but not everything is good for you. And even though "I am allowed to do anything," I must not become a slave to anything. You say, "Food was made for the stomach, and the stomach for food." (This is true, though someday God will do away with both of them.) But you can't say that our bodies were made for sexual immorality. They were made for the Lord, and the Lord cares about our bodies." 1 Corinthians 6:12-13 NLT

"Run from sexual sin! No other sin so clearly affects the body as this one does. For sexual immorality is a sin against your own body. Don't you realize that your body is the temple of the Holy Spirit, who lives in you and was given to you by God? You do not belong to yourself, for God bought you with a high price. So you must honor God with your body." 1 Corinthians 6:18-20 NLT

"For I am afraid that when I come I won't like what I find, and you won't like my response. I am afraid that I will find quarreling, jealousy, anger, selfishness, slander, gossip, arrogance, and disorderly behavior. Yes, I am afraid that when I come again, God will humble me in your presence. And I will be grieved because many of you have

not given up your old sins. You have not repented of your impurity, sexual immorality, and eagerness for lustful pleasure. This is the third time I am coming to visit you (and as the Scriptures say, "The facts of every case must be established by the testimony of two or three witnesses"). I have already warned those who had been sinning when I was there on my second visit. Now I again warn them and all others, just as I did before, that next time I will not spare them. I will give you all the proof you want that Christ speaks through me. Christ is not weak when he deals with you; he is powerful among you. Although he was crucified in weakness, he now lives by the power of God. We, too, are weak, just as Christ was, but when we deal with you we will be alive with him and will have God's power. Examine yourselves to see if your faith is genuine. Test yourselves. Surely you know that Jesus Christ is among you; if not, you have failed the test of genuine faith." 2 Corinthians 12:20 – 13:5 NLT

"Let there be no sexual immorality, impurity, or greed among you. Such sins have no place among God's people." Ephesians 5:3 NLT

"And I remind you of the angels who did not stay within the limits of authority God gave them but left the place where they belonged. God has kept them securely chained in prisons of darkness, waiting for the great day of judgment. And don't forget Sodom and Gomorrah and their neighboring towns, which were filled with immorality and every kind of sexual perversion. Those cities were destroyed by fire and serve as a warning of the eternal fire of God's judgment." Jude 6-7 NLT

"But you, my dear friends, must remember what the apostles of our Lord Jesus Christ predicted. They told you that in the last times there would be scoffers whose purpose in life is to satisfy their ungodly desires. These people are the ones who are creating divisions among you. They follow their natural instincts because they do not have God's Spirit in them." Jude 16-19 NLT

The above Scriptures are just a few of the many passages of God's Holy Word on this subject. This is the Word of the Lord, despite how we may personally feel about it. It is God's Holy Law. Many of our traditional national Laws are based on Holy Law, but we are now witnessing the rise of those who are determined to overturn and re-write our traditional Laws, relentlessly pushing for Governments to implement what they demand in the name of 'equality'. Whether or not our national leaders agree with the cultural climate of our times, it would seem that new Laws are being made on the basis of/ and to appease the cries of 'political correctness'.

The Purpose of the Church

The purpose of the Church is to welcome all who come in. We are to preach to everyone that God's grace, mercy and forgiveness towards us as sinners is for **now**, this day and every single day, until the Day of Judgment. The Church must then show **all** who come into God's House, His truth about themselves and their lifestyles from His Holy Word, and then counsel and disciple them into clean and holy living, obeying Jesus' command to "Go, and sin no more" (see John 8:11).

Everyone who comes into God's House as an unbeliever enters as a sinner, defiled by the beliefs and practices of their unbelieving lifestyle, whatever these may be. The desire of our heart for coming into God's House should be because we are convicted of our sins and our need of salvation. We know deep inside that we cannot change ourselves, nor can we save ourselves. We need to be delivered from the inherent disposition of sin that is in us so that we can then begin to live clean, righteous and holy lives in thankfulness to Jesus for what He has done for us on the Cross, for our salvation. This happens through confession and repentance, where we receive God's forgiveness for our sins.

Our purpose and motive for entering God's House should be solely to worship Him with humble and grateful hearts, desiring to serve Him and please Him by obeying His Word.

Paul's letter to the Philippians says,

"Dear friends, you always followed my instructions when I was with you. And now that I am away, it is even more important. Work hard to show the results of your salvation, obeying God with deep reverence and fear. For God is working in you, giving you the desire and the power to do what pleases him." Philippians 2:12-13 NLT

If we claim that we love Jesus and that we are His followers, then this Scripture says that we **will work hard** to show the results of our salvation by **obeying God** with deep reverence and fear. But if our desires and powers are to do what is **contrary** to His Word, then it is not God who is working in us, but in fact it is the enemy of God; yes, Satan and his demons. We can be sure that our rebellious desires are not pleasing to God because we are not obeying Him with deep reverence and fear.

This passage goes on to say,

"Live clean, innocent lives as children of God, shining as bright lights in a world full of crooked and perverse people. Hold firmly to the word of Life;" (v15b-16a).

So, as followers of Christ, are we living clean and innocent lives in this world full of crooked and perverse people? Or are our lives as crooked and perverse as the world around us, almost indistinguishable from the lifestyles of the culture of our times?

Are we holding firmly to the word of life, or are we part of the rising band of people in the Church whose lives display that they have no desire to follow Christ at all, but in fact wish to live lives of open defiance and rebellion against His word of life? Are we amongst those whose purpose is to resist, reject and counter God's Word and cause division within the Church, insisting on pushing and coercing those in authority in the Church to 'reinterpret' Holy Scripture and remove supposedly 'offending' passages from the Church's preaching and teaching?

This rising band of rebellious followers of Christ may succeed in removing from Church doctrine many of the Scriptures that they don't like or don't agree with, but they will never remove it from the Bible. What is written in the Bible is God's Word of Life, and it will stand for eternity, despite the protests of many who are against what is written.

The Lord created all humanity and He sees everything that we do. We think we can mock God and remain defiant against His Holy Word, but the passage below shows that, at the end of the day, we are nothing but a frail blade of grass that He will blow away with the breath of His mouth. **But** His Word will **stand forever**. The Lord spoke this to the prophet Isaiah,

"A voice says, "Call out [prophesy].""
Then he answered, "What shall I call out?"
[The voice answered:] All humanity is [as frail as] grass, and all
that makes it attractive [its charm, its loveliness] is [momentary]
like the flower of the field.
The grass withers, the flower fades, when the breath of the LORD
blows upon it;
Most certainly [all] the people are [like] grass.
The grass withers, the flower fades,
But the word of our God stands forever." Isaiah 40:6-8 AMP

Therefore, if we claim to be a follower of Christ, we should not receive God's mercy, grace and forgiveness lightly. If we think that we can enter God's House and can carry on in our sinful practices after we have come to the knowledge of the truth, we are utterly deceived.

The Letter to the Hebrews makes this fact unmistakeable.

"Dear friends, if we deliberately continue sinning after we have received knowledge of the truth, there is no longer any sacrifice that will cover these sins. There is only the terrible expectation of God's judgment and the raging fire that will consume his enemies." Hebrews 10:26-27 NLT

The apostle Paul says to followers of Christ in Rome,

"But because you are stubborn and refuse to turn from your sin, you are storing up terrible punishment for yourself. For a day of anger is coming, when God's righteous judgment will be revealed. He will judge everyone according to what they have done." Romans 2:5-6 NLT

Again, Paul says,

"Do not let any part of your body become an instrument of evil to serve sin. Instead, give yourselves completely to God, for you were dead, but now you have new life. So use your whole body as an instrument to do what is right for the glory of God." Romans 6:13 NLT

To the believers in Corinth, he says,

"Run from sexual sin! No other sin so clearly affects the body as this one does. For sexual immorality is a sin against your own body. Don't you realize that your body is the temple of the Holy Spirit, who lives in you and was given to you by God? You do not belong to yourself, for God bought you with a high price. So you must honor God with your body." 1 Corinthians 6:18-20 NLT

And to the believers in Ephesus, Paul gives instruction on Christian living, saying,

"So I tell you this, and insist on it in the Lord, that you must no longer live as the Gentiles do, in the futility of their thinking. *They are darkened in their understanding and separated from the life of God because of the ignorance that is in them due to the hardening of their hearts.* **Having lost all sensitivity, they have given themselves over to sensuality so as to indulge in every kind of impurity, and they are full of greed.**

That, however, is not the way of life you learned when you heard about Christ and were taught in him in accordance with the truth that is in Jesus. You were taught, with regard to your former way of life, to put off your old self, which is being corrupted by its deceitful desires; to be made new in the attitude of your minds; and

to put on the new self, created to be like God in true righteousness and holiness." Ephesians 4:17-24 NIV (author's emphasis)

Chambers puts it like this:

"...do I realise that my "body is the temple of the Holy Spirit," or am I condoning some habit in my body which clearly could not stand the light of God on it? (1 Corinthians 6:19). God formed His Son in me through sanctification, setting me apart from sin and making me holy in His sight (see Galatians 4:19). But I must begin to transform my natural life into spiritual life by obedience to Him. God instructs us even in the smallest details of life. And when He brings you conviction of sin, do not "confer with flesh and blood" but cleanse yourself from it at once (Galatians1:16). Keep yourself cleansed in your daily walk.

I must cleanse myself from all filthiness in my flesh and my spirit until both are in harmony with the nature of God. Is the mind of my spirit in perfect agreement with the life of the Son of God in me, or am I mentally rebellious and defiant? Am I allowing the mind of Christ to be formed in me? (see Philippians 2:5). Christ never spoke of His right to himself, but always maintained an inner vigilance to submit His spirit continually to His Father. I also have the responsibility to keep my spirit in agreement with His Spirit." (Excerpt from March 18th) [3]

But many in the Church, both leaders and the flock, are rebellious and defiant, saying, "Our bodies are our own, and we will do what we like with them. Stop telling us that we are sinning against God." In view of the Scriptures above, how can we possibly say it is okay to do what we like with our bodies, let alone actually believe such a lie?

The apostle John says to believers,

"If we say that we have fellowship with Him and yet walk in the darkness [of sin], we lie and do not practice the truth;" 1 John 1:6 AMP

This Scripture makes it clear that we **only** have fellowship with God **if** we are walking in the **light** of God's truth. We cannot be involved in the deeds of darkness (anything that is contrary to God's Word) and still believe we are okay with God. We are deceiving ourselves with Satan's lies.

The apostle Paul gives clear instructions to the Church concerning what should be done when followers of Christ persist in sexual sin. The following passage seems to be one that is seriously ignored in the Church today.

"When I wrote to you before, I told you not to associate with people who indulge in sexual sin. But I wasn't talking about unbelievers who indulge in sexual sin, or are greedy, or cheat people, or worship idols. You would have to leave this world to avoid people like that. I meant that you are not to associate with anyone who claims to be a believer yet indulges in sexual sin, or is greedy, or worships idols, or is abusive, or is a drunkard, or cheats people. Don't even eat with such people. It isn't my responsibility to judge outsiders, but it certainly is your responsibility to judge those inside the church who are sinning. God will judge those on the outside; but as the Scriptures say, "You must remove the evil person from among you." 1 Corinthians 5:9-13 NLT

Is this happening in your Church? Do your church leaders deal with habitual, unrepentant sin in this firm way? The way things look in our current Church culture is that sexual sin is now being ignored, often tolerated and condoned, and at worst it is being embraced and encouraged more and more as something that is a loving thing to allow and accept in the Church, for the sake of unity and inclusivity.

Scripture clearly teaches that followers of Christ who persist in unrepentant sin should be put out of the church. However, there is hope for them to return and be restored to the body of Christ. If at some point they then come to their senses and repent of their sin and change their behaviour, they can then be welcomed back into the fellowship of the church (see 2 Corinthians 2:5-8).

As we read in one of the passages above, Jude 16-19, when we satisfy our ungodly desires, following our natural instincts and thereby creating divisions in the Church, it is because we do not have the Spirit of God in us. If we do not have God's Spirit then we do not belong to God, and we are not a follower of Christ, no matter how much we may profess and insist that we are.

The apostle Paul confirms this in the following passage.

"That's why those who are still under the control of their sinful nature can never please God. But you are not controlled by your sinful nature. You are controlled by the Spirit if you have the Spirit of God living in you. (And remember that those who do not have the Spirit of Christ living in them do not belong to him at all.)" Romans 8:8-9 NLT

Paul also says to the believers at Corinth,

"The person without the Spirit does not accept the things that come from the Spirit of God but considers them foolishness, and cannot understand them because they are discerned only through the Spirit." 1 Corinthians 2:14 NIV

If we are still under the control of our sinful nature, we do not have the Spirit of God living in us, and so the Word of God will be 'foolishness' to us and we will resist it, disobey it, and reject it. This being the case, how can we still insist that we have the Spirit of God in us and that we belong to God, and how can we expect or even hope that our soul will go to heaven when we die? We are deceiving ourselves.

If we have no desire to repent of our sins, we have no business being in God's House, and no right to call ourselves a follower of Christ.

However, it is evident today, by what we are seeing being taught in the Church, that many who are leading our churches and preaching from the pulpit **do not** have the Spirit of God in them. The Scriptures above say that these people do not belong to God. Yet we are allowing them to teach us and lead us!

If they do not have God's Spirit and do not belong to God and the Kingdom of Light, then the one they belong to is Satan and his kingdom of darkness. These people teach doctrines that are of the Antichrist. They teach that it is okay to come into God's House and disobey His Word, and remain in habitual, unrepentant sin, still choosing to ignore God's Word and His verdict on sin.

But on the Day of Judgment, God's Word will be our judge. The Day of the Lord will change everything. His mercy and grace will cease, and His judgment will begin.

The Day of Judgment

When we are standing before the Judgment seat of Christ, making excuses and trying to justify our actions and our defiant rebellion, I believe that Jesus will remind us of all those who, over the years, have tried hard to warn us to repent of our sins, and He will undoubtedly say to us,

"It is written…"

… and will then proceed to remind us of all that God's Word says about unrepentant sin, and will show us the eternal destiny of all who have rejected and disobeyed His Word. All of our excuses will be futile, and our eternal 'appointment' with hell will be irrevocable.

How will we feel then?

If you don't want this to happen to you, please continue to read this book, and then read chapter 6, and pray the prayer at the end of that chapter. Your eternal destiny hangs in the balance. What you do with what God's Word has revealed to you is something that should not be ignored any longer.

I am praying for all within the Church who have been impacted by the convicting Word of the Lord. Jesus is calling you to repent, now, for none of us knows if we will even have a tomorrow. I exhort you this day; do not turn away from the grace of God. Come to your senses, return to your heavenly Father, confess your sins and receive His mercy, His forgiveness and His restoration. Then leave your life of sin, and begin to live a life of godliness, as an offering of thanks to the Lord for His sacrifice of love for you in Jesus.

g) 'Pop-culture' style of worship

It seems that in much of the Church, we have entered an era where we feel that the only way we will ever get people into the Church is to offer them a style of worship that is more like a worldly 'gig' than a time of reverential worship to our Holy God. The current style of worship is designed to attract today's unbelievers and younger people. Yes, some of this is good and can be reverential, but there is also a lot going on which is making it hard to distinguish church worship bands from the bands of the secular world.

An example which is in the public domain, is the story of a man believed to be a Mega-church's youth pastor, whose 'on-stage' gimmick was to dress as the 'Naked Cowboy', performing to a packed audience at a women's conference in not much more than a pair of boxer shorts and a cowboy hat. It is not clear if he was actually leading worship or if this was just a bit of 'fun' to hype up the audience prior to the actual time of worship. Regardless of this, this kind of thing should not be happening in any Church setting. Whilst the leaders of this mega-church have given an apology for this deplorable event, all I can say is, "What would Jesus think?"

Have we lost our minds? Where is our reverential fear of the Holiness of God? What are we doing using worldly gimmicks to attract and hype up the audience?

Have we forgotten that Jesus is in the midst of us? We need to ask ourselves, "Would Jesus want me to be doing this? Is what I am doing pleasing God and bringing glory to Him?" If not, STOP DOING IT!

Come on Church, Wake Up!

The examples of **false gospels** that I have listed on all the previous pages are just a few of the things that are occurring in the Church today, under the label of 'Christianity'. These things do not stand up under the scrutiny of the Holy Word of God, and are therefore counterfeits of authentic Christianity.

If you are amongst this kind of deception, flee from all forms of it urgently. Your eternal destiny depends on it.

ii) False Messiahs

Followers of Christ know that Jesus is going to return, but what is hard to comprehend is that they could actually be deceived into believing that Jesus has **already** come back! Are these believers reading their Bibles? Have they not read Jesus' warnings regarding false messiahs in the passages that I highlighted in chapter 2 of this book?

It is shocking to discover that there are many who are being deceived like this. False messiahs are popping up around the world and are drawing in thousands of people who claim to be Christians. These people are longing for Jesus' return, but sadly they have taken their eyes off God's Word.

Their desperate longing to see Jesus has caused them to become vulnerable to evil-minded people, whose sole desire is to rise up and claim that they are Jesus, and to have people follow them and worship them, and believe their false teachings.

An Internet search will reveal many of these false messiahs, but here are just a few.

People currently claiming to be the 'Second Coming' of Jesus.

1. A man named Sergey Anatolyevitch Torop, known as Vissarion to his followers, leads a cult known as 'The Church of the Last Testament', which is situated in the Taiga forest in Siberia.

He looks like the 'Jesus' that the media portray, and has many followers. He even has his own website. There are videos of this leader on YouTube.

2. Sung Myung Moon, the leader of the Unification Church.

3. Jose Luis de Jesus Miranda, founder and leader of 'Growing in Grace International Ministry Inc.', who claims he is 'the man Jesus'. Bizarrely, he claims to be both Jesus Christ returned **and** the Antichrist, and has the numbers 666 tattooed on his arm.

4. A man named Baha'u'llah, who has declared to be the 'promised One' of all religions, claiming to be several 'messiahs' converging into one person, symbolically.

5. On YouTube, there are many videos of a magician named 'Dynamo', who is drawing large crowds with his performance of tricks that are in the realms of 'signs and wonders'. Whilst not claiming to be the Messiah, this man uses trickery to 'walk on water', and in one of his tricks, he 'ascends' up into the air in front of the statue of Jesus on the top of Sugarloaf Mountain, in Rio de Janeiro, in front of stunned onlookers.

This magician's tricks may just be the tip of the iceberg; Jesus warned His first disciples that in the 'times of the end', false messiahs and false Christs would rise up and perform great signs and wonders to deceive people, even God's chosen ones (see Matthew 24:24 & Mark 13:22). We are seeing these things come to pass in our current generation, and we should heed Jesus' warnings, and not get caught up in believing and following the crowds that flock to these deceptions.

It is one thing, as a follower of Christ, to try to walk on water, like Peter did, when Jesus called him to get out of the boat and walk to Him (see Matthew 14:22-32). Peter was looking to Jesus in faith, to enable him to walk on the water. But it is something very different to take supernatural abilities that belong to Jesus, and turn them into 'magic tricks' to draw in crowds and fool them.

Brothers and sisters-in-Christ, do not follow anyone who appears in these times, proclaiming that they are the Second Coming of Christ. The Scripture below tells us exactly how Jesus will return, and for sure this event has not occurred yet!

"After saying this, he was taken up into a cloud while they were watching, and they could no longer see him. As they strained to see him rising into heaven, two white-robed men suddenly stood among them. "Men of Galilee," they said, "why are you standing here staring into heaven? Jesus has been taken from you into heaven, but someday he will return from heaven in the same way you saw him go!" Acts 1:9 -12 NLT

Nor be deceived by anyone performing Biblical 'signs and wonders' when they are simply doing magic tricks to 'wow' the crowds, and where the performer gives no glory to God for these 'signs and wonders'.

iii) 'Date-setters' for the Rapture, Second Coming & End of the World

Over the past few years the Internet has become awash with End Time 'date-setters', with people proclaiming that the Lord has given them dates and times for the rapture, His Second Coming, and even the end of the world. A search on YouTube will bring up a long list of videos that people have made on this subject.

I believe that there are many people who are being given genuine dreams and visions by the Lord regarding the rapture, the Second Coming and the end of the world, in order to wake the Church up, and they are writing books about them or posting them on YouTube. The genuine books and videos are the ones that do not set dates for the occurring of these events, but are simply alerting people to be watchful and ready for His appearing, so that we will know when it is 'at the door' (see Matthew 24:33 & Mark 13:29).

The Bible says that in the End Times, people will have dreams and visions (see Joel 2:28- 29), and I know this to be true because the Lord plagued me with such dreams for a period of four years, which I mention in my book *The End of the World and What Jesus Has to Say About It*.

I have also read several genuine books on these 'yet to be fulfilled' events, one powerful book being *'Last Call for the Church'* by Patricia C. McGlennon, which covers the endlessly debated issue of the Rapture. I have listed this in the Recommended Reading section at the back of this book.

Over the years I have been tossed to and fro by the Church's confusion about the Rapture, and so I prayed about it and asked the Lord to clarify it to me. I had no idea how the Lord would do this, so I just left it with Him. A few days after I prayed about it, He gave me a very vivid dream of the Rapture. As is Biblically correct, the Lord did not give me a date for its occurrence, but below is my sincere and very personal account of the dream – which I will never forget. It encouraged me immensely at a time when I was extremely weary of the effort to keep going, and so my prayer is that it will encourage you too, to keep hold of your faith and to remain steadfast on this journey until He comes.

My Dream of the Rapture

The Lord gave me a very powerful dream where I was suspended high up in the heavens and I was looking down at the Earth.

My eyes were riveted on a tiny speck, and it was as if my eyes had super-fast lenses that zoomed down on this speck on the Earth. As my vision zoomed in, I saw that the speck was me in my physical body which was standing on the Earth. My physical self was standing with my eyes closed tight and my face raised up to heaven, just like it says in the Scripture, "Lift up your heads for your redemption draweth nigh." (Luke 21:28)

I was still watching myself from high up in the heavens when, all of a sudden, a tremendous power and intense light came from the heavenly realms, which felt like a huge vacuum suction, almost like the vortex of a tornado. I watched as this power and light shot down from heaven to Earth at a speed that I simply cannot describe, and it was heading straight towards me on the Earth.

As it got closer to me, my whole being began to shake and vibrate and I was not able to remain standing on the Earth any longer. Gravity was not able to hold me down on the Earth, and all of a sudden, I was caught up in this powerful force, and I was drawn up into the heavens at lightning speed.

Then I woke up…

I have no doubt that the Lord has given me this dream of the Rapture. So many in the Church do not believe this will take place. I believe it will take place, and so I asked the Lord to confirm the truth to me. He chose to answer my question by giving me a very personal dream of it, which I am truly grateful for.

With the way things are upon the Earth in these present times, I personally am almost desperate for the Lord to return and pray that it would be soon. My hope is that many in the Church will feel the same, but sadly much of the Bride of Christ has fallen 'asleep' whilst waiting for her Bridegroom to return for her.

But what I want to warn readers of here is the fact that Satan can see our desperation and has latched on to this, and is even sowing deception into people's dreams of the rapture, the Second Coming and the end of the world where they are predicting **specific dates** for the occurring of these events.

No Man Knows the Day or the Hour

Jesus has said that no man knows the day or the hour, nor the angels, not even Jesus Himself, but only the Father knows (see Matthew 24:36). In view of this, whilst people may be having dreams of the rapture, Second Coming and the end of the world, and posting them on the Internet and Social Media, we must ignore and avoid any that predict dates for these events, because they are Satan's counterfeits. We must not believe or follow anything or anyone who predicts dates for what Jesus does not even know about! To say that we have been given a specific date for these things is to exalt ourselves above Jesus. Remember who tried to exalt himself above God? ...Yes, SATAN!

We can be sure that those who do this are false prophets, whom Jesus has told us to ignore. So anyone who predicts specific dates for the rapture, the Second Coming, or the end of the world is a liar sent by Satan to deceive and cause believers to fall away in the last days from the true Gospel of Jesus Christ.

Over the years I am sure we have all heard of the names of various people and religious organisations who have predicted and proclaimed dates for Jesus' return and the end of the world. When that date has arrived and Jesus has not returned, they just dismiss it as a simple miscalculation, without any explanation for their errors, and then they set a new 'predicted date'!

Examples

The following are just a few examples of people who have been 'date-setters', and some of these show the disastrous consequences of their deception.

An Internet search will reveal that:

i) in 1843 William Miller predicted that Jesus would return sometime between 1843-1844;

ii) in 1876 Charles Taze Russell, founder of the Jehovah's Witnesses, predicted the great day of the Lord would be in 1914. Since then the Society has predicted many other dates for Jesus' return, all of which have failed;

iii) Harold Camping, who predicted the end of the world to be on May 21st 2011 and when that failed he amended it to October 21st 2011.

There are more up to date failed predictions on YouTube, and there are many others who have made predictions throughout the centuries.

But some false prophets have even deceived their 'followers' with teaching that they must commit suicide if Jesus fails to return on their predicted date.

Again, an Internet search reveals that:

i)   in 1978, Jim Jones claimed to be a reincarnation of Jesus and ordered his 900 followers to commit suicide by drinking a concoction containing cyanide;

ii) in 1993, David Koresh also claimed he was God, and he and 80 of his followers burned to death in the siege that took place in Waco, Texas;

iii) in 1997, Marshall Applewhite, another self-proclaimed Messiah and the leader of the Heavens Gate sect, organised for his 38 followers to commit suicide.

These kinds of situations surely have to be religious deception at its worst.

These examples are awful, but they are only a few.

The world is seeing the fulfilment of Jesus' warnings of the rise in false prophets. Do not listen to the lies of these people, who deceive you with doctrine that contradicts God's Holy Word, or you will become ensnared in false doctrine and false religion, with disastrous eternal consequences.

God's Word makes it very clear that **no one** will know the day or the hour of Jesus' return (see Matthew 25:13). Our part is to **keep watch** for the biblical signs of the approaching end, and to warn each other to make ourselves ready for that Day, not to exalt ourselves to a position of prophesying or predicting dates for the

Rapture, or Jesus' Second Coming, or the end of the world as we know it, when to do so is completely contrary to the Word of God.

When we claim to be able to predict the date for these end times events, we are actually claiming to know information that only God knows. This type of activity is the deceiving work of Satan, and it is leading millions of people to follow the 'puffed-up' declarations of these false prophets. There is only one place such predictions will lead to, and that is eternity in hell for all who continue to believe the lies of these false prophets whom Satan is using upon the earth. Heed God's warnings and flee from such teaching.

iv) New World Order and One World Religion

Under this heading, it is not my intention to write in any detail on this subject. There is much to be found on this subject, on the Internet, and YouTube, as well as several books. One particular book that I believe is absolutely essential reading for all who profess to be followers of Christ is *Trumpet Blast Warning* by Jason Carter. Two chapters in his book are dedicated to the New World Order and the One World Religion. His book certainly lives up to its title!

So, in this section, I will highlight very briefly what I have found through an Internet search, using the sources I listed at the beginning of this chapter, as well as other public domain material, and will leave you to delve further.

My searching on this subject revealed that it seems that the Vatican's desire is to create a New World Order with a One World Religion, for the sake of 'religious unity' and 'world unity and peace'. Meetings have been held, with many World leaders and heads of religious institutions and spiritual organizations in attendance, including leaders of the 'Emerging Church' of our times.

The articles suggest that the meetings hope to persuade these high-profile leaders, from all forms of 'faith', to embrace the ideology of this New World Order/One World Religion. With media coverage and reporting of these meetings, and the spin that is put on them for the 'peace and security' of the global population, at some point it would then be easy to put their ideology into effect.

Merging the 'faiths'

Some Internet articles show that there could be a merging of Christianity and Islam, creating a 'unified' religion called 'Chrislam'. In fact, there are articles which state that Berlin is to build the first 'Chrislam Church', called 'The House of One', which will be an all-in-one mosque, church and synagogue, where Muslims, Christians and Jews can come together to worship and pray, albeit in separate designated areas. But how long will it be before the three are merged together into the 'unity' of a One World Religion?

So, is this New World Order/One World Religion some far-fetched, unrealistic ideology? Not according to God! This End Times global superpower with its global religion is written about in the Book of Revelation, chapters 13 & 17.

This scenario is coming upon the earth, and as followers of Christ, we need to study God's Word on it, and remain steadfast to His Word when the pressure ramps up for us to compromise and conform for the sake of so-called unity.

A World Without Cash; and the Microchip

Internet searches shows that it is also the desire of the New World Order to create what is being openly called a 'cashless society', where all financial transactions are done through technology contained in a microchip device inserted in our hand. This technology, known as the RFID chip, already exists and is being implemented in various countries under the guise of being used for 'safety' or 'security'.

It is currently being 'advertised' by the media as the best way to keep track on children and other vulnerable people, such as the elderly; this might indicate that at some point all children and elderly people could be 'chipped'. Other articles suggest that at some point, we will all have this microchip, containing all our medical information, for quick access by health care providers in medical emergencies.

Some Internet sites reveal media 'advertising' for shops to exist where people can pay for their goods by waving their micro-chipped hand across the scanner on their way out of the shop. There is even a mainstream media article by the BBC, dated 29th January, 2015, on the RFID chip, titled, *Office Puts Chip Under Staff's Skin*.

If all this sounds horrifying, well it should do! This sounds very much like the 'Mark of the Beast' mentioned in the Book of Revelation (see Revelation 13:16-18), where no one will be able to buy or sell anything unless they have this 'mark' in their right hand or in their forehead.

Several books have been written on the subject of the Mark of the Beast and the Cashless Society; *The End of Money* and *Cashless*, both by Mark Hitchcock, are just two of them. Also, *Trumpet Blast Warning* by Jason Carter has a chapter on the Mark of the Beast.

In a world of ever-increasing technology, it is a constant temptation to have the latest 'gadget'. Many of the younger generation in the Church seem to think it is 'cool' to have a world where cash is no longer needed, and do not seem to think twice about having 'contactless' bank cards. Personally, I think we **do** need to think twice about these things, as each gadget that is advertised as the next thing in 'technological progress', is a step nearer to the mandatory insertion of the RFID chip into our hands.

Much of the Church has no idea what God's Word says on these issues, and many leaders remain silent about them when in fact they should be warning believers, in the strongest possible terms, of what is coming upon the earth.

So, this chapter on Satan's counterfeits is simply to alert us to what is going on in the Church today, particularly under the labels of 'Church' and 'Christianity', and to sound the alarm bells as to what is just around the corner for humanity in general. It is sad to say that many believers are not aware of this, or even interested. I know this to be true in my own circles. Only a few seem to be 'awake' to what is going on, but many professing followers of Christ look at me as if I am deranged for saying such things.

It troubles me deeply that many believers are not keeping a Biblical watch concerning the End Times, as Jesus has warned us to do, and even scoff at the suggestion that they are asleep and need to wake up.

When followers of Christ respond in this way to God's Word, it seems that many are walking on a different path to what His Word exhorts them to follow.

So, if we are not walking on God's path, which path are we on?

Chapter 5

WHICH PATH ARE YOU ON?

Jesus said,

"You can enter God's Kingdom only through the narrow gate. The highway to hell is broad, and its gate is wide for the many who choose that way. But the gateway to life is very narrow and the road is difficult, and only a few ever find it." Matthew 7:13-14 NLT

a) The Wide Gate that leads to Destruction

As I have tried to show throughout this book, counterfeit Christianity is a broad path of many false 'gospels' peddled by many false prophets and false messiahs, and following these counterfeits will lead you through the wide gate to hell.

In addition to the passage of Scripture at the head of this chapter, let's read some short verses from the Word of God, showing what awaits all who remain on Satan's highway to hell. There are many more passages of Scripture that I could add, but in the interest of space in this book, I will keep this list as it is, and encourage you to undertake your own search for further Biblical confirmation of the awful realities of hell for all who are walking on Satan's path.

"Don't be afraid of those who want to kill your body; they cannot touch your soul. Fear only God, who can destroy both soul and body in hell." Matthew 10:28 NLT

"And shall cast them into a furnace of fire: there shall be wailing

and gnashing of teeth." Matthew 13:42 KJV

"Then said the king to the servants, 'Bind him hand and foot, and take him away, and cast him into outer darkness, there shall be weeping and gnashing of teeth.'" Matthew 22:13 KJV

"And shall cut him asunder, and appoint him his portion with the hypocrites: there shall be weeping and gnashing of teeth." Matthew 24:51 KJV

"Now throw this useless servant into outer darkness, where there will be weeping and gnashing of teeth." Matthew 25:30 NLT

"But whoever causes one of these little ones who believe in Me to stumble, it would be better for him if a millstone were hung around his neck, and he were thrown into the sea. If your hand causes you to sin, cut it off. It is better for you to enter into life maimed, rather than having two hands, to go to hell, into the fire that shall never be quenched — where

> *'Their worm does not die*
> *And the fire is not quenched.'*

And if your foot causes you to sin, cut it off. It is better for you to enter life lame, rather than having two feet, to be cast into hell, into the fire that shall never be quenched — where

> *'Their worm does not die,*
> *And the fire is not quenched.'*

And if your eye causes you to sin, pluck it out. It is better for you to enter the kingdom of God with one eye, rather than having two eyes, to be cast into hell fire — where

> *'Their worm does not die*
> *And the fire is not quenched.'* Mark 9:44-48 NKJV

"There shall be weeping and gnashing of teeth, when ye shall see Abraham, and Isaac, and Jacob, and all the prophets, in the kingdom of God, and you yourselves thrust out." Luke 13:28 KJV

"For God did not spare even the angels who sinned. He threw them into hell, in gloomy pits of darkness, where they are being held until the day of judgment." 2 Peter 2:4 NLT

*"Look, I will come as unexpectedly as a thief! Blessed are all who are watching for me, who keep their clothing ready so they will **not have to walk around naked and ashamed.**"* Revelation 16:15 NLT (author's emphasis)

"And anyone whose name was not found recorded in the Book of Life was thrown into the lake of fire." Revelation 20:15 NLT

"Blessed are those who wash their robes. They will be permitted to enter through the gates of the city and eat the fruit from the tree of life. Outside the city are the dogs — the sorcerers, the sexually immoral, the murderers, the idol worshipers, and all who love to live a lie." Revelation 22:14-16 NLT

The Reality of Hell

These are just **some** of the passages in the Bible concerning the reality of eternity in hell for all who claim to be followers of Christ, but whose lives display more that they are followers of Satan. There are many more passages in the Gospels, but I have not included them here as many of them repeat what is written in the verses I have listed above.

These passages are not my words; they are the Words of Jesus Himself.

We can choose to ignore them, but to do so is to deny God and His Son Jesus Christ, even if we still claim to be His followers. The Day of Judgment will reveal the truth.

So, if you know that you are on this path - the highway to hell - I urge you to repent, **now**, for the sake of your eternal destiny. You are playing 'Russian Roulette' with the salvation of your soul. God does not want any to perish, but for all to come to repentance so that they can be saved (see 2 Peter 3:9).

But it is up to us to make this choice. God will not force us to. We are the ones who must choose between heaven and hell. God has given us the free gift of eternal life through His Son Jesus Christ. It is up to us to accept His gift, and to live our lives with faith in Jesus. If we reject His gift, then eternity in hell will be our destination.

With this dreadful reality in store for all who are walking on the broad path to destruction, I plead with you to read the next chapter of this book, 'Where do we go from here?' It is not too late! The Lord is gracious and merciful, full of compassion for all who truly repent. We must realise how far we have wandered from His path, and turn around and run back to Him, with godly sorrow, and confess and repent of our sins. He will receive us with love and forgiveness, cleansing us from our sins (see 1 John 1:9).

b) The Narrow Gate that leads to Eternal Life

If we are not following Satan's counterfeits, but instead are obeying God's Holy Word, with daily repentant hearts, hating the sins which can so easily beset us, and desiring to lay them aside (see Hebrew 12:1), and are keeping watch for the 'signs of the times' and the return of our Bridegroom, then this is the Narrow Gate that leads to Life.

The following Scriptures show what awaits all who are walking on the road that leads to Life.

[Speaking to His twelve disciples] *"Jesus replied, "I assure you that when the world is made new and the Son of Man sits upon his glorious throne, you who have been my followers will also sit on twelve thrones, judging the twelve tribes of Israel. **And everyone who has given up houses or brothers or sisters or father or mother or children or property, for my sake, will receive a hundred times as much in return and will inherit eternal life."*** Matthew 19:28-29 NLT (author's emphasis)

"And then at last, the sign that the Son of Man is coming will

*appear in the heavens, and there will be deep mourning among all the peoples of the earth. And they will see the Son of Man coming on the clouds of heaven with power and great glory. **And he will send out his angels with the mighty blast of a trumpet, and they will gather his chosen ones from all over the world — from the farthest ends of the earth and heaven.**"* Matthew 24:30-31 NLT (author's emphasis)

"His master replied, 'Well done, good and faithful servant! You have been faithful with a few things; I will put you in charge of many things. Come and share your master's happiness!'" Matthew 25:23 NIV

"Then the King will say to those on his right, 'Come, you who are blessed by my Father; take your inheritance, the kingdom prepared for you since the creation of the world.'" Matthew 25:34 NIV

"Do not let your hearts be troubled. You believe in God; believe also in me. My Father's house has many rooms; if that were not so, would I have told you that I am going there to prepare a place for you? And if I go and prepare a place for you, I will come back and take you to be with me that you also may be where I am." John 14:1-3 NIV

"But now that you have been set free from sin and have become slaves of God, the benefit you reap leads to holiness, and the result is eternal life. For the wages of sin is death, but the gift of God is eternal life in Christ Jesus our Lord." Romans 6:22-23 NIV

"For if you live according to the flesh, you will die; but if by the Spirit you put to death the misdeeds of the body, you will live. For those who are led by the Spirit of God are the children of God... Now if we are children, then we are heirs — heirs of God and co-heirs with Christ, if indeed we share in his sufferings in order that we may also share in his glory... I consider that our present sufferings are not worth comparing with the glory that will be revealed in us." – Romans 8:13-14, 17-18 NIV (author's emphasis)

"And do this, understanding the present time: The hour has already come for you to wake up from your slumber, because our salvation is nearer now than when we first believed." Romans 13:11 NIV

"No eye has seen, no ear has heard, and no mind has imagined what God has prepared for those who love him." 1 Corinthians 2:9 NLT

*"I declare to you, brothers and sisters, that flesh and blood cannot inherit the kingdom of God, nor does the perishable inherit the imperishable. **Listen, I tell you a mystery: We will not all sleep, but we will all be changed — in a flash, in the twinkling of an eye, at the last trumpet. For the trumpet will sound, the dead will be raised imperishable, and we will be changed. For the perishable must clothe itself with the imperishable, and the mortal with immortality.**"* 1 Corinthians 15:50-53 NIV (author's emphasis)

"Therefore we do not lose heart. Though outwardly we are wasting away, yet inwardly we are being renewed day by day. For our light and momentary troubles are achieving for us an eternal glory that far outweighs them all. So we fix our eyes not on what is seen, but on what is unseen, since what is seen is temporary, but what is unseen is eternal." 2 Corinthians 4:16-18 NIV

*"For we know that if the earthly tent we live in is destroyed, **we have a building from God, an eternal house in heaven, not built by human hands. Meanwhile we groan, longing to be clothed instead with our heavenly dwelling, because when we are clothed, we will not be found naked.** For while we are in this tent, we groan and are burdened, because we do not wish to be unclothed but to be clothed instead with our heavenly dwelling, **so that what is mortal may be swallowed up by life. Now the one who has fashioned us for this very purpose is God, who has given us the Spirit as a deposit, guaranteeing what is to come.** Therefore we are always confident and know that as long as we are at home in the body we are away from the Lord. For we live by faith, not by sight. **We are confident, I**"*

say, and would prefer to be away from the body and at home with the Lord. So we make it our goal to please him, whether we are at home in the body or away from it. For we must all appear before the judgment seat of Christ, so that each of us may receive what is due us for the things done while in the body, whether good or bad." 2 Corinthians 5:1-10 NIV (author's emphasis)

"For, as I have often told you before and now tell you again even with tears, many live as enemies of the cross of Christ. Their destiny is destruction, their god is their stomach, and their glory is in their shame. Their mind is set on earthly things. **But our citizenship is in heaven. And we eagerly await a Savior from there, the Lord Jesus Christ who, by the power that enables him to bring everything under his control, will transform our lowly bodies so that they will be like his glorious body."** Philippians 3:18-21 NIV (author's emphasis)

"Once you were alienated from God and were enemies in your minds because of your evil behavior. But now he has reconciled you by Christ's physical body through death to present you holy in his sight, without blemish and free from accusation — **if you continue in your faith, established and firm, and do not move from the hope held out in the gospel."** Colossians 1:21-23(a) NIV (author's emphasis)

"And now, dear brothers and sisters, we want you to know what will happen to the believers who have died so you will not grieve like people who have no hope. For since we believe that Jesus died and was raised to life again, we also believe that when Jesus returns, God will bring back with him the believers who have died. We tell you this directly from the Lord: we who are still living when the Lord returns will not meet him ahead of those who have died. **For the Lord himself will come down from heaven with a commanding shout, with the voice of the archangel, and with the trumpet call of God. First, the Christians who have died will rise from their graves. Then, together with them, we who are still alive and remain on the earth will be caught up in the clouds to meet the Lord in the air. Then we**

will be with the Lord forever. So encourage each other with these words." 1 Thessalonians 4:13-18 NLT (author's emphasis)

*"I have fought the good fight, I have finished the race, I have kept the faith. **Now there is in store for me the crown of righteousness, which the Lord, the righteous Judge, will award to me on that day — and not only to me, but also to all who have longed for his appearing."*** 2 Timothy 4:7-8 NIV (author's emphasis)

*"But when the kindness and love of God our Savior appeared, he saved us, not because of righteous things we had done, but because of his mercy. He saved us through the washing of rebirth and renewal by the Holy Spirit, whom he poured out on us generously through Jesus Christ our Savior, **so that, having been justified by his grace, we might become heirs having the hope of eternal life."*** Titus 3:4-7 NIV (author's emphasis)

*"But he has appeared once for all at the culmination of the ages to do away with sin by the sacrifice of himself. Just as people are destined to die once, and after that to face judgment, so Christ was sacrificed once to take away the sins of many; **and he will appear a second time, not to bear sin, but to bring salvation to those who are waiting for him."*** Hebrews 9:26b-28 NIV (author's emphasis)

"Blessed is the one who perseveres under trial because, having stood the test, that person will receive the crown of life that the Lord has promised to those who love him." James 1:12 NIV

*"Praise be to the God and Father of our Lord Jesus Christ! In his great mercy he has given us new birth into a living hope through the resurrection of Jesus Christ from the dead, **and into an inheritance that can never perish, spoil or fade. This inheritance is kept in heaven for you, who through faith are shielded by God's power until the coming of the salvation that is ready to be revealed in the last time.** In all this you greatly rejoice, though now for a little while you may have had to suffer grief in all kinds of trials. These have come so that the proven genuineness of your faith — of greater worth than gold, which perishes even though refined by fire — may result*

in praise, glory and honor when Jesus Christ is revealed. **Though you have not seen him, you love him; and even though you do not see him now, you believe in him and are filled with an inexpressible and glorious joy, for you are receiving the end result of your faith, the salvation of your souls.**" 1 Peter 1:3-9 NIV (author's emphasis)

"*Therefore, my brothers and sisters, make every effort to confirm your calling and election. For if you do these things, you will never stumble, and you will receive a rich welcome into the eternal kingdom of our Lord and Savior Jesus Christ.*" 2 Peter 1:10-11 NIV

"*Dear friends, now we are children of God, and what we will be has not yet been made known. But we know that when Christ appears, we shall be like him, for we shall see him as he is. All who have this hope in him purify themselves, just as he is pure.*" 1 John 3:2-3 NIV

"*Whoever has ears, let them hear what the Spirit says to the churches. To the one who is victorious, I will give the right to eat from the tree of life, which is in the paradise of God.*" Revelation 2:7 NIV

"*Whoever has ears, let them hear what the Spirit says to the churches. To the one who is victorious, I will give some of the hidden manna. I will also give that person a white stone with a new name written on it, known only to the one who receives it.*" Revelation 2:17 NIV

"*To the one who is victorious and does my will to the end, I will give authority over the nations — that one 'will rule them with an iron scepter and will dash them to pieces like pottery' — just as I have received authority from my Father. I will also give that one the morning star.*" Revelation 2:26-28 NIV

"*All who are victorious will be clothed in white. I will never erase their names from the Book of Life, but I will announce before my Father and his angels that they are mine.*" Revelation 3:5 NLT

"*All who are victorious will become pillars in the Temple of my God, and they will never have to leave it. And I will write on them the name of my God, and they will be citizens in the city of my God — the new Jerusalem that comes down from heaven from my God. And I will also write on them my new name."* Revelation 3:12 NLT

"Those who are victorious will sit with me on my throne, just as I was victorious and sat with my Father on his throne." Revelation 3:21 NLT

"Look, I am coming soon! My reward is with me, and I will give to each person according to what they have done. I am the Alpha and the Omega, the First and the Last, the Beginning and the End. Blessed are those who wash their robes, that they may have the right to the tree of life and may go through the gates into the city." Revelation 22:12-14 NIV

All glory be to God for our wonderful inheritance!

The Difficult Road

But, as Jesus said in the passage at the head of this chapter, for those who are walking on the road to Life, the "road is difficult", and because of this, many followers of Christ are abandoning His path to Life, hoping to enter the Kingdom of Heaven by an 'easier' route.

Wake up! There **is no** easier route! The only other path is the **highway to hell**!

As followers of Christ, we must continue to walk on the difficult road to eternal Life. Whatever comes our way whilst we are on our journey to our eternal home in the Kingdom of Heaven, we must overcome the trials and tribulations that will undoubtedly occur.

Concerning the "difficult road", Chambers says,

"If we are going to live as disciples of Jesus, we have to remember that all efforts of worth and excellence are difficult. The Christian life is gloriously difficult, but its difficulty does not make us faint and cave in – it stirs us up to overcome. Do we appreciate the miraculous

salvation of Jesus Christ enough to be our utmost for His highest - our best for His glory? ... Thank God that He does give us difficult things to do! His salvation is a joyous thing, but it is also something that requires bravery, courage and holiness. It tests us for all we are worth. Jesus is "bringing many sons to glory" (Hebrews 2:10), and God will not shield us from the requirements of sonship. God's grace produces men and women with a strong family likeness to Jesus Christ, not pampered, spoiled weaklings. It takes a tremendous amount of discipline to live the worthy and excellent life of a disciple of Jesus in the realities of life. And it is always necessary for us to make an effort to live a life of worth and excellence." (Excerpt from July 7th) [1]

In each of Jesus' letters to the seven churches in the Book of Revelation, He tells the churches what awaits all those who repent and overcome. Jesus' words of promise are for **all** who faithfully follow Him, not just the believers to whom those letters were written.

I am sure most of us will know or have read John Bunyan's classic story *Pilgrims Progress*. This is the story of the individual journey we must make from the kingdom of darkness to the Kingdom of Light. We will encounter much temptation and many attacks from Satan and his demons whilst we are on the path to the 'Celestial City', but we must remain faithful to God and His Holy Word so that we will be able to keep walking on the narrow and difficult path to Life.

I have read a wonderful version of this book, written over fifty years ago for the younger generation, so that they could enjoy Bunyan's classic in more modern language. It is so captivating that, even though it is written for children, when I read it myself, at the age of about forty, I could not put it down! It is titled *Little Pilgrim's Progress*, written by Helen L. Taylor. I have listed this book in the Recommended Reading section at the back of this book.

So, dear faithful pilgrims, let us march on with faith and obedience, until we reach our heavenly home! All the trials that we encounter on our journey will vanish in the brightness of God's glory, and we will hear Him say to us,

"Well done, good and faithful servant; you were faithful over a few things, I will make you ruler over many things. Enter into the joy of your lord." Matthew 25:21 NKJV

And also,

"Come, you who are blessed by my Father; take your inheritance, the kingdom prepared for you since the creation of the world." Matthew 25:34 NLT

… and we will fall down and worship Him forever.

Chapter 6

WHERE DO WE GO FROM HERE?

So, having got this far in the book, if we profess to be followers of Christ but are caught up in sinful ways which we have not repented of, and/or are following Satan's counterfeit 'gospels' – anything that is contrary to God's Word - we are left with the choice of continuing to live in sin, or obeying God's Word; between spending eternity in hell or eternity in heaven.

The choice is ours.

Taken again from his classic, *My Utmost for His Highest*, Chambers says,

"We have to recognise that sin is a fact of life, not just a shortcoming. Sin is blatant mutiny against God, and either sin or God must die in my life" (Excerpt from June 23rd) [1]

"In the teachings of Jesus Christ the element of judgment is always brought out – it is a sign of the love of God. Never sympathize with someone who finds it difficult to get to God; God is not to blame. It is not for us to figure out the reason for the difficulty, but only to present the truth of God so that the Spirit of God will reveal what is wrong. The greatest test of the quality of our preaching is whether or not it brings everyone to judgment. When the truth is preached, the Spirit of God brings each person face to face with God Himself." (Excerpt from May 5th) [2]

"There is no heaven that has a little corner of hell in it. God is

determined to make you pure, holy, and right, and He will not allow you to escape the scrutiny of the Holy Spirit for even one moment. He urged you to come to judgment immediately when He convicted you, but you did not obey. Then the inevitable process began to work, bringing its inevitable penalty. Now you have been "thrown into prison, [and]...you will by no means get out of there till you have paid the last penny" (Matt 5:25-26). Yet you ask, "Is this a God of mercy and love?" When seen from God's perspective, it is a glorious ministry of love. God is going to bring you out pure, spotless, and undefiled, but He wants you to recognize the nature you were exhibiting – the nature of demanding your right to yourself. The moment you are willing for God to change your nature, His recreating forces will begin to work. And the moment you realise that God's purpose is to get you into the right relationship with Himself and then with others, He will reach to the very limits of the universe to help you take the right road." (Excerpt from July 1st) [3]

"For one who is born again, it is easier to live in a right-standing relationship with God than it is to go wrong, provided we heed God's warnings and "walk in the light"(1 John 1:7)." (Excerpt from December 24th) [4]

Heeding God's Warnings

Notice in the passage above, the words "provided we heed God's warnings and 'walk in the light'". As followers of Christ, we will only stay on God's path to eternal life if we obey His Word, walk in the light, and heed His warnings whenever we begin to doubt or go astray. Anything other than this is 'wishful thinking', and we deceive ourselves if we think it is okay to believe and follow any old 'wind of doctrine' in the vain hope that we will still be permitted entry into the Kingdom of Heaven.

On the subject of "walking in the light", Chambers says,

"I must "walk in the light as he is in the light..." – not in the light of my own conscience, but in God's light. If I will walk there, with

nothing held back or hidden, then this amazing truth is revealed to me: "...the blood of Jesus Christ His Son cleanses [me] from all sin" so that God Almighty can see nothing to rebuke in me. On the conscious level it produces a keen, sorrowful knowledge of what sin really is. The love of God working in me causes me to hate, with the Holy Spirit's hatred for sin, anything that is not in keeping with God's holiness." (Excerpt from December 26th) [5]

Let's continue with some more Scriptures.

"For the kind of sorrow God wants us to experience leads us away from sin and results in salvation. There's no regret for that kind of sorrow." 2 Corinthians 7:10 NLT

"Do not let sin control the way you live; do not give in to sinful desires. Do not let any part of your body become an instrument of evil to serve sin. Instead, give yourselves completely to God, for you were dead, but now you have new life. So use your whole body as an instrument to do what is right for the glory of God. Sin is no longer your master, for you no longer live under the requirements of the law. Instead, you live under the freedom of God's grace.

Well then, since God's grace has set us free from the law, does that mean we can go on sinning? Of course not! Don't you realize that you become the slave of whatever you choose to obey? You can be a slave to sin, which leads to death, or you can choose to obey God, which leads to righteous living. Thank God! Once you were slaves of sin, but now you wholeheartedly obey this teaching we have given you. Now you are free from your slavery to sin, and you have become slaves to righteous living." Roman 6:12-18 NLT

This is a powerful passage of Scripture!

Life or Death – The Choice is Ours

It is clear from the passage above that, even as followers of Christ, we can choose to still be a slave to our sins, but doing so will **lead to death** (spiritual death). Or we can choose to obey God, which leads to righteous living.

Firstly, let's assume that we are members of churches that **are** teaching God's Word without compromising it in any way. If that is the case, we should now be doing what Paul says to the believers in Rome:

"Once you were slaves of sin, **but now you wholeheartedly obey this teaching we have given you.***"* Romans 6:17 NLT (author's emphasis).

So we need to ask ourselves this question:

"Am I, as an individual, wholeheartedly obeying the teaching that has been given to me?"

As followers of Christ, if we examine our hearts and our lives before God, and we find that the answer to this question is "No", then we must do something about it as a matter of urgency. The salvation of our soul is not something we can procrastinate about. None of us knows when we are going to die. If we die tomorrow, and we have been messing about in the world, with our feet walking on the highway to hell, it will be too late to repent. Our eternal destiny in hell will be sealed. Nothing will change this reality.

But today, yes this very day...

i) It's not too late!

For believers caught up in unrepentant sin

If you are a follower of Christ who is caught up in un-confessed and unrepentant sin, I urge you to pray to the Lord the prayer I have written a little later in this section, from the depth of your heart.

I do not know what you may be struggling with or to what depths you are caught up in sin, but I would like you to know that I have struggled with unrepentant and repetitive sin, as a follower of Christ. God in His great mercy has shown me how much He loves me by revealing to me my un-confessed and unrepentant sin, disciplining me to confess it and repent of it, so that I could receive His cleansing, forgiveness and restoration.

That truly is the love of God! He could have left me in my sinful mess and abandoned me to the consequences of my sinful choices: eternity in hell. But instead, His incredible love reached down to me in my un-confessed mess, and chastened and disciplined me to repent of it all out of His awesome heart of love! This process is extremely painful but equally filled with indescribable grace, forgiveness, freedom, joy and peace! Praise God!

If we truly want to serve the Lord, and we know that what we are doing, whether secretly or openly, is not in keeping with His Holy Word, the Lord will reveal our sins to us, and will convict us of our sin and unrighteousness so that we can do something about it. He knows our eternal destiny if we do not heed His warnings. However, God still leaves us with the freewill to either heed His warnings or choose not to.

As I have mentioned throughout this book, if we refuse to yield to God and obey His Word, when He has shown us the way, it is our choice that determines our eternal destiny. God holds open His offer of mercy, forgiveness and reconciliation to us, right up to the moment that we draw our last breath. But after that, there is no more opportunity to repent…only judgment.

Repent and Return to the Bridegroom

So, if you believe in Jesus Christ but have got yourself caught up in sin - anything that is contrary to God's Word – and you are trying to justify it as something that is okay to do and are not accepting and admitting that it is sinful, I urge you now to heed God's warnings to do so. Repent and return to the Bridegroom. It may be the last opportunity that you get, as none of us knows when our last breath will be.

Come humbly before the Lord in brokenness and shame for the sins you have allowed yourself to drift in to. Do this with sincerity, wanting to be rid of the habits and lifestyle that have deceived and enticed you away from obedience to the Holy Word of God.

God longs for you to spend eternity with Him in heaven. It is His heart's desire that you enter the City Gates so that He can say to you,

"Well done my good and faithful servant!" (Matthew 25:23) and, *"Come, you who are blessed by my Father; take your inheritance, the Kingdom prepared for you since the creation of the world."* (Matthew 25:34)

But the Word of God has shown us repeatedly that only those believers who live their lives in Christ in obedience to His Word will inherit eternal life. No believer who rejects God's verdict on sin will be allowed into the Kingdom of Heaven.

So, at this critical point, you are faced with the choice to yield to God's truth about your continual unrepentant sins, and confess and repent of them now, or to continue as you are – in rebellion to the Word of God.

I urge you to confess and repent now.

The apostle Paul's letter to the **believers** in Rome confirms clearly that we should not keep on sinning:

"Yes, Adam's one sin brings condemnation for everyone, but Christ's one act of righteousness brings a right relationship with God and new life for everyone. Because one person disobeyed God, many became sinners. But because one other person obeyed God, many will be made righteous. God's law was given so that all people would see how sinful they were. But as people sinned more and more, God's wonderful grace became more abundant. So just as sin ruled over all people and brought them to death, now God's wonderful grace rules instead, giving us right standing with God and resulting in eternal life through Jesus Christ our Lord. Well then, should we keep on sinning

so that God can show us more and more of His wonderful grace? Of course not! Since we have died to sin, how can we continue to live in it?" Romans 5:19-6:2 NLT

Further, Paul's letter to Titus also confirms this:

"For the grace of God that brings salvation has appeared to all men. It teaches us to say "No" to ungodliness and worldly passions, and to live self-controlled, upright and godly lives in this present age, while we wait for the blessed hope – the glorious appearing of our great God and Saviour, Jesus Christ, who gave himself for us to redeem us from all wickedness and to purify for himself a people that are his very own, eager to do what is good." Titus 2:11-14 NIV

Again, Paul says the same things to the Thessalonian **believers**:

"It is God's will that you should be sanctified: that each of you should learn to control his own body in a way that is holy and honourable, not in passionate lust like the heathen, who do not know God." 1 Thessalonians 4:3-5 NIV

And again,

"For God did not call us to be impure, but to live a holy life. Therefore, he who rejects this instruction does not reject man but God, who gave you His Holy Spirit." 1 Thessalonians 4:7-8 NIV

To the **believers** in the Ephesian church, Paul writes:

"But among you there must not be even a hint of sexual immorality, or of any kind of impurity, or of greed, because these are improper for God's holy people. Nor should there be obscenity, foolish talk or coarse joking, which are out of place, but rather thanksgiving. For of this you can be sure: no immoral, impure or greedy person – such a man is an idolater – has any inheritance in the Kingdom of Christ and of God. Let no one deceive you with empty words, for because of such things God's wrath comes on those who are disobedient. Therefore do not be partakers with them." Ephesians 5:3-7 NIV

The Lord God spoke similar words through the prophet Isaiah:

"Wash and make yourselves clean. Take your evil deeds out of my sight! Stop doing wrong, learn to do right!" Isaiah 1:16-17(a) NIV

And finally, listen to what the Lord told the prophet Jeremiah to speak to His people:

"'Don't be fooled into thinking that you will never suffer because the Temple is here. It's a lie! Do you really think you can steal, murder, commit adultery, lie, and burn incense to Baal and all those other new gods of yours, and then come here and stand before me in my Temple and chant, "We are safe!" — only to go right back to all those evils again? Don't you yourselves admit that this Temple, which bears my name, has become a den of thieves? Surely I see all the evil going on there. I, the LORD, have spoken!'" Jeremiah 7:8-11 NLT

So if you are a believer caught up in un-confessed and unrepentant sin, and you want to get yourself right with God so that you can start living your life in readiness for Jesus' return, with the hope of eternal life in heaven, I encourage you to pray the following prayer or a similar one as the Holy Spirit leads you.

ii) A Prayer of Confession and Repentance

"Father, I come before You with the mess that I have made of my life. At some point, I have allowed myself to be deceived by Satan's counterfeits to the true and authentic Christianity as revealed in Your Holy Word. I have allowed myself to be enticed into sinful thoughts and sinful behaviour, and I have continually made excuses for these; foolishly believing that I would still inherit eternal life despite being involved in sinful practices that I have not confessed and repented of.

"Thank You for loving me so much by revealing to me the deceptions that I have been believing and following, and also my un-confessed and unrepentant sins. Thank you for revealing to me the awful eternal consequences that will occur if I continue living in these ungodly ways.

"Father, right now, I confess every one of my sins that I am struggling with and am caught up in, which I have not repented of.

(I suggest that you list all of your un-confessed and unrepentant sins, and name them out loud to the Lord in this prayer.)

"Lord, I confess out loud to You into the heavenly realms, that I have sinned in all these ways and have grieved You by participating in them. I am truly sorry Lord, and I ask for Your forgiveness and cleansing through the precious blood of Jesus Christ.

"As of this day, I renounce all my involvement in these sins; I repent of them and turn back to Christ. I do not want to participate in sinful practices anymore and I ask You, Lord, to help me and convict me in the future, and use the correcting rod of Your Holy Word if I begin to stray again, so that I can quickly come back onto the straight and narrow path that leads to eternal life.

"This day, I declare before all of heaven that I want to live my life in obedience to the Holy Word of God. I want to yield to the Lord's will and choose to do what is acceptable and pleasing in His sight, and to resist temptation's enticement to fall back into sin again.

"Your Word says that, *"Godly sorrow leads to repentance which leads to salvation."* (2 Corinthians 7:10).

"I confess that I have stubbornly made excuses for my sins and have rejected Your Word that says I need to have godly sorrow about them.

"Father, in Your love for me, I ask that You would create in me a heart that is truly sorry, with a godly sorrow, for the sins I have committed whilst I self-righteously upheld my right to still call myself a believer.

"Let me know what it means to feel and fully experience the godly sorrow that leads to repentance, which leads to salvation. My heart and my life need a complete transformation, and only You, Lord, are able to do this in me.

"I give all that I am to You this day, Father. I am Your prodigal child who has mucked around in the pigsty of the world, but now I have finally come to my senses and am returning back to my Father's house in confession and repentance of my sins. Let me fall into Your loving arms of forgiveness and be fully restored in my relationship with You (see the story of the prodigal son in Luke 15:11-31).

"Thank You Father, for loving us so much that You have left the gate wide open for Your wayward children to return to You when they stray into sin. This gate is the gate of confession and repentance, which You have mercifully revealed to me, and which I humbly accept and acknowledge as the truth, in order to receive Your forgiveness, cleansing and restoration.

"Father, please give me a deep hunger and thirst to read and obey Your Word, and to no longer compromise with it when faced with temptation to sin.

"Help me to remain rooted and grounded in the truth of Your Word, so that my life will be continually pleasing to You. I want to be diligent and steadfast in reading, obeying, and applying Your Word, and to persevere and overcome to the end, so that I will hear the words I long to hear, saying, *"Well done, My good and faithful servant!"* and *"Come, you who are blessed by My Father; take your inheritance, the Kingdom prepared for you since the creation of the world"* (see Matthew 25:21, 34).

"This is the most precious possession that anyone could ever inherit, and I truly want to receive it.

"I offer this prayer to You Father, with thanksgiving and faith, in the name of my Lord and Saviour Jesus Christ. Amen."

From This Day Forward

If you have prayed this prayer, rise up and walk away from your life of sin, and determinedly and diligently obey God's Word from this day forward. Flee from every form of sin and evil.

Many good churches have designated staff who are responsible for pastoral care and counselling, so I encourage you to seek help from them and make yourself accountable to someone who is mature in the faith and is obedient to God's Word, asking for his or her help to keep you on track.

Pray daily, and fill your mind and your soul with God's precious Word. If the church you go to is preaching a counterfeit gospel, leave that place and ask the Lord to lead you to a church that is obeying His Word.

Take control of your life and bring it into captivity to obey the Word of God, every minute of the day.

"The weapons we fight with are not the weapons of the world. On the contrary, they have divine power to demolish strongholds. We demolish arguments and every pretension that sets itself up against the knowledge of God, and we take captive every thought to make it obedient to Christ." 2 Corinthians 10:4-5 NIV

There is a constant battle raging in the spiritual realm for your soul and its eternal destiny. You must do your part to keep walking on the difficult path to the Kingdom of Heaven. The Lord is with you, and He will help you. He says to you,

"Whether you turn to the right or to the left, your ears will hear a voice behind you, saying, 'This is the way; walk in it.'" Isaiah 30:21 NIV

"Stop at the crossroads and look around.
  Ask for the old, godly way, and walk in it.
Travel its path, and you will find rest for your souls."
Jeremiah 6:16 NLT

Listening to the leading of the Holy Spirit and obeying God's Word will keep you on the difficult path to the Kingdom of Heaven. God's Word has never said that following Him would be easy, but the eternal rewards for being faithful and obedient followers of Christ will far outweigh everything that our life of faith on this earth has had to endure for His sake.

"And since we are his children, we are his heirs. In fact, together with Christ we are heirs of God's glory. But if we are to share his glory, we must also share his suffering. Yet what we suffer now is nothing compared to the glory he will reveal to us later." Romans 8:17-18 NLT

Let this blessed Word of the Lord encourage you.

Chapter 7

THE WATCHMAN'S FINAL PLEA

Over the past decade, I have noticed the gradual compromise of Biblical standards that has been occurring in the content published in some Christian magazines, which were once prepared to stand steadfast to God's Word, printing articles that upheld God's Word.

But, due to the influence of the 'political correctness' of the times we now live in, some magazines are now openly publishing articles highlighting teachings and practices among believers that are diametrically opposed to God's Holy Word.

As if such subtle 'promotion' is not bad enough, magazines that do this do not appear to be countering these false teachings by upholding God's view of what is being promoted and accepted within the Church these days. They seem to leave the content of their articles 'open', for readers to decide for themselves what they want to believe and follow.

Many followers of Christ are being exposed to and deceived by compromising, ungodly material, which is being dressed up to look 'spiritual'. This is occurring not just in so-called 'Christian' magazines, but also at Christian camps, conferences, Colleges and Universities, and, as this book has shown, in the Church environment in general.

It is therefore even more vital in these times of great deception that the truth of God's Word should be spoken **in** and **amongst** a world full of counterfeits. How will those who say they are followers of Christ, who are being exposed to counterfeits, ever know the truth unless someone speaks God's truth to them?

We must be valiant warriors for the Lord, speaking His truth to today's compromising Church, letting His Word shine brightly in a world full of deception and increasing darkness.

Brothers and sisters-in Christ, it is without doubt that we are living in times of great turmoil and deception **within** the Church (as well as in the world). Almost two-thousand years ago, Jesus warned His followers of what would be coming on the earth, with the appearance of false gospels, false prophets and false messiahs, as well as signs in the heavens and on the earth.

In my book *The End of the World and What Jesus Has to Say About It*, I did my best to deliver God's message to wake people up to these escalating 'signs of the times', frequently described as 'unprecedented' and 'apocalyptic' by the media.

In that book, I touched on a few things to do with false gospels and false messiahs, but after it was published I felt the Lord compelling me to write this new book, to wake the Church up to the serious and eternal dangers of counterfeit Christianity.

There is so much more that I could write on various aspects, but the purpose of this book is to sound the trumpet warning of danger, to alert the Church to wake up to the reality of counterfeit Christianity. It is the responsibility of each follower of Christ to heed God's warnings and to do what He says.

As we read at the front of this book, in the passage of 'God's Watchman' in Ezekiel 33:1-9, the watchman's responsibility is to deliver the message to the people, but he is not responsible for their eternal destiny if they do not respond to the message.

Time is running out!

There is so much happening in the world today, which fulfils

Bible Prophecy, and Jesus has exhorted us to look for the signs of His soon return.

Deception and apostasy in the Church are major signs, and, as I end this book, I am even more saddened today by the latest Breaking News from the BBC (16th February, 2017). Despite a report given by the House of Bishops, concerning the issue of whether to allow same-sex marriages to be conducted in the Church, and also blessing ceremonies of same-sex unions, where the House of Bishops' counsel is that the Church should stop short of progressing in this direction, the result is that the general Synod of the Church of England have voted not to take note of the Bishops' report.

This is the latest example of the shepherds of the Church rejecting God's Word, and relentlessly pushing to have Church doctrine changed to include the desires of those within the Church who refuse to accept God's Word as it is. But as each day goes by, social media articles show that this sort of thing is happening within the Church with more and more frequency.

An online search will also reveal further examples of those within the Church who are openly declaring that they are living lifestyles that are contrary to God's Word, but rather than accept His Word, they want the Church to change their doctrine and 'move with the times'.

A huge reality check is needed here: The Church is not supposed to 'move with the times'! The Church is meant to preach the truth of God's Word, and uphold the truth in the face of the rising tsunami of deception that is crashing against its doors. In many churches, this tsunami has succeeded in breaking down the doors, and its torrent of deception is washing away God's truth from the House of God, and what is left is an unrepentant den of iniquity. They then push to create a new style of 'church' based on their ungodly desires.

Instead of faithfulness and obedience to God's Word, a culture of rebellion is rising within the Church, which rejects God's Word and any 'God-ordained' authority, and will not stop until its 'desires' are fulfilled.

This sort of thing will escalate as time goes on, until the Day of the Lord appears. We are in the times of End Times apostasy – the Great Falling Away (see 2 Thessalonians 2:3), the times of the rise of false teachers and false gospels.

... The times of 'counterfeit Christianity'.

If we proclaim to be a follower of Christ and have fallen for these deceptions, Jesus wants us to wake up and come to our senses, then run back to Him in repentance, before it is too late.

A few weeks ago, a friend of mine, Pam, woke up in the early hours of the morning. She felt the Holy Spirit giving her a message and compelling her to write it down. When I met up with her a couple of days ago, she gave me the note and said that she felt the Lord wanted her to give it to me. When I read the note, the Holy Spirit pierced my heart because of the message it contained, and the need for it to be put in this book. I told her about the feeling inside me from the Holy Spirit, and she has given me her permission to include the message. The following is what she wrote down.

"Stay close, read My Word. My Word will bring light and expose strategies of the enemy. **Seducing spirits have been released.** Things aren't always what they appear. The enemy appears as an angel of light. Not all supernatural is of God. **Those that are deceived do not realise it.** Beware of ungodly affiliations. Test the spirits. Ask for wisdom and discernment. Plead the blood of Jesus always. Be led into all truth. **There will be great deception over all the earth.** My sheep hear my voice. Be not afraid. I will lead you and protect you. The devil prowls around like a roaring lion, to see who he may devour. Pray in tongues. Deep calls to deep."

Thank you Pam, for being obedient to the Lord and writing down His message in the middle of the night. He is speaking to His children to warn the Church of the flood of seducing spirits that are drowning this sheep.

As I close this book, I pray that all who have read it, and are touched and challenged by its message, will this very day take advantage of God's mercy and grace, which is only available this side of the Day of Judgment. Ask the Lord to bring His loving gift of conviction upon you to confess and repent of your waywardness, and turn back to Him in obedience to His Holy Word. He **will** forgive those who **truly** repent (see Luke 24:47(b)).

The apostle Paul said to the believers at Corinth,

"For we must all appear before the judgment seat of Christ, so that each of us may receive what is due us for the things done while in the body, whether good or bad." 2 Corinthians 5:10 NIV

Paul also says to them,

"As God's co-workers we urge you not to receive God's grace in vain. For he says,

"In the time of my favor I heard you, and in the day of salvation I helped you." I tell you, now is the time of God's favor, now is the day of salvation." 2 Corinthians 6:2 NIV

Every day that goes by, where we are wallowing around in the pigsty of counterfeit Christianity, is another day where we are walking on the highway to hell.

Jesus says,

"Look, I am coming soon, bringing my reward with me to repay all people according to their deeds." Revelation 22:12 NLT

"Blessed are those who wash their robes. They will be permitted to enter through the gates of the city and eat the fruit from the tree of life." Revelation 22:14 NLT

A time is soon coming when it will be too late, and judgment will begin.

The apostle Paul says,

"But because you are stubborn and refuse to turn from your sin, you are storing up terrible punishment for yourself. For a day of anger is coming, when God's righteous judgment will be revealed. He will judge everyone according to what they have done." Romans 2:5-6 NLT

"Dear friends, if we deliberately continue sinning after we have received knowledge of the truth, there is no longer any sacrifice that will cover these sins. There is only the terrible expectation of God's judgment and the raging fire that will consume his enemies." Hebrews 10:26-27 NLT

*"He will come with his mighty angels, in flaming fire, bringing judgment on those who don't know God **and on those who refuse to obey the Good News of our Lord Jesus.** They will be punished with eternal destruction, forever separated from the Lord and from his glorious power."* 2 Thessalonians 1:7-9 NLT (author's emphasis)

So, dearly beloved of the Lord, let us 'wash our robes' before the Lord, with repentant hearts full of godly sorrow, that we may receive His mercy and forgiveness **now**, whilst the Day of Salvation is still here for all to receive.

I will end with a personal testimony of something that happened to me recently, during the writing of this book. The God-incident that occurred brings all that I have written to a fitting conclusion.

Testimony

During a time of prayer in my 'closet' recently, I was restless, and was struggling to find words to pray concerning the burdens that have been a part of my daily life for the past twenty-five years in Christ. I felt the Lord lovingly say, "Sing to Me!"

I reached over to the bookshelf and pulled out a hymnbook. I said to the Lord, "What do you want me to sing?" I allowed the book to fall open 'at random' and said to myself that I would sing whatever was on the page.

When I was a child, we frequently sang a famous old hymn at school, but I absolutely detested singing it because of the repetitive and fast pace at which the music was played, and so the words of the hymn never impacted me. It is awful to confess this, but I have detested the hymn for fifty years.

So, there I was, in my 'closet' with the hymnbook in my hands, and it fell open to this very hymn! With intense feelings of arrogance, I slammed the hymnbook shut, and said to God, "I am NOT singing THAT!"

Without hesitation, the Lord rebuked me for my sinful response. His loving request to sing to Him was now turned to a **command**; "SING TO ME!"

I felt utterly ashamed for my arrogance towards this hymn, and I asked the Lord to forgive me. Again I heard Him sternly say, "SING TO ME", so I opened the hymnbook again, and stared at the page. At that moment, my soul was flooded with a different tune to the one we had sung at school.

I began to sing slowly the first sentence of the first verse, with the tune that was racing round in my soul. I became so overwhelmed with tears of deep emotion that it took me about ten minutes to actually sing all the verses.

Every single sentence of the hymn was so powerful, speaking to me of my journey of faith as one of God's 'pilgrims', reassuring me that the Lord is with me to the very end. The hymn reflects deeply the story in John Bunyan's *Pilgrims Progress*.

The whole purpose of my life in Christ is to serve Him to the end, amidst all that may come my way along the journey, with my hope and trust in God that, at the end, He will receive me into His kingdom.

This hymn is truly the heart of the message of this book, which you are holding in your hands, and have finally reached the end of.

With this testimony in mind, below is the hymn, which I once intensely detested, but now I sing almost every day. I cannot sing it without weeping. I recently sang it over and over in my mind one night, to help me fall asleep…and it worked!

Glory to God for this wonderful hymn!

In some music books, the tempo for the tune, which the Lord brought to my mind, is described as 'bold', but in the music book that I have, the tempo is indicated as 'slow'. I encourage you to sing it slowly, as I personally found that this has a more profound effect upon my soul.

You could do an Internet search to hear this tune played, although it may be played in the 'bold' tempo!

I have listed the title of the tune below.

O, Jesus I Have Promised (J.E Bode 1816-1874)[1]

(Tune: 'Thornbury' – Basil Harwood 1859-1949)[2]

O Jesus, I have promised
To serve thee to the end;
Be thou forever near me,
My Master and my Friend;
I shall not fear the battle
If thou art by my side,
Nor wander from the pathway
If thou wilt be my Guide.

O let me feel thee near me:
The world is ever near;
I see the sights that dazzle,
The tempting sounds I hear;
My foes are ever near me,
Around me and within;

But, Jesus, draw thou nearer,
And shield my soul from sin.

O let me hear thee speaking
In accents clear and still,
Above the storms of passion,
The murmurs of self-will;
O speak to reassure me,
To hasten, or control;
O speak, and make me listen,
Thou Guardian of my soul.

O Jesus, thou hast promised
To all who follow thee,
That where thou art in glory
There shall thy servant be;
And, Jesus, I have promised
To serve thee to the end;
O give me grace to follow
My Master and my Friend.

O let me see thy footmarks,
And in them plant mine own;
My hope to follow duly
Is in thy strength alone;
O guide me, call me, draw me,
Uphold me to the end;
And then in heaven receive me,
My Saviour and my Friend.

NOTES

Chapter 1

1. Oswald Chambers, *My Utmost for His Highest,* ed. James Reimann (Grand Rapids, MI: Discovery House, 1992) April 10th entry.

Chapter 4

1. Chambers, December 19th entry.
2. Chambers, December 29th entry.
3. Chambers, March 18th entry.
4. Chambers, December 8th entry.

Chapter 5

1. Chambers, July 7th entry.

Chapter 6

1. Chambers, June 23rd entry.
2. Chambers, May 5th entry.
3. Chambers, July 1st entry.
4. Chambers, December 24th entry.
5. Chambers, December 26th entry.

Testimony

1. J.E. Bode (1816-1874), *O, Jesus I Have Promised* (Public Domain)

2. Basil Harwood (1859-1949) 'Thornbury' (Public Domain in the U.S)

RECOMMENDED READING

Michael L. Brown, *Go and Sin No More*
ISBN 978-0-615-73019-6

Jason Carter, *Beyond Earthly Realms*
ISBN 978-0-992795214

Jason Carter, *Trumpet Blast Warning*
ISBN 978-0-9927952-0-7

Darren Hibbs, *The Year of The Lord's Favor?*
ISBN 978-09889195-1-8

Rev. Jack Munley, *The Church in America is Dying...But is all Hope Lost?* ISBN 978-1-4984-1149-3

Patricia C. McGlennon, *Last Call for the Church*
ISBN 978-1456515218

J.C. Ryle, *Are You Ready for The End of Time? Understanding future events from prophetic passages of the Bible*
ISBN 1-85792-747-8

Helen L. Taylor, *Little Pilgrim's Progress*
ISBN 978-0802447999

Nancy Ravenhill, *Touched by Heaven*
ISBN 978-0-8007-9604-4

ABOUT THE AUTHOR

Although I was born on the Isle of Wight in 1961, I have lived a very nomadic life, having lived in over thirty houses since my birth! Four of those years were spent at a boarding school.

At the age of nine we lived in Gibraltar for about two years, which was a wonderful experience as a child.

Throughout my life, I have believed God existed and I knew that Jesus had died on a cross, but that was as far as my faith went, despite being confirmed at boarding school at the age of thirteen, and having attended many different churches over the past thirty years.

No one explained to me until 1992 that, in the eyes of God, I was a sinner and was in need of salvation. Once this had been explained to me, the following day I was baptised by full immersion in water and was filled with the Holy Spirit and spoke in tongues, just like the first disciples did on the Day of Pentecost!

God had reached down and changed me from a broken, depressed and suicidal wreck, transforming me into a person full of the joy of the Lord. I knew that God had done something dramatic inside me through my new faith in Jesus Christ.

The Lord has performed many healing miracles in my life and the lives of others whom I have prayed for in His authority and in His name.

However, through many wrong choices I have regrettably made in my life in Christ, my growth in faith suffered many setbacks over the past twenty years. But thankfully, in October 2011, God in His great mercy, reached down and extended His hand of grace and love to me, and showed me exactly what my un-confessed and unrepentant sins look like in His sight.

This was a deeply gruelling experience, but the fruit of this pain produced my first book *Come on Church! Wake Up!* published in January 2013.

I thank the Lord for the experience He took me through and is still taking me through each day. My life has become very different to how it was previously. All the things that consumed my life and my time, I no longer crave to do anymore. This aspect was a sudden transformation brought about by the Holy Spirit, following the Lord revealing to me that the time I spent doing these things was causing me to neglect my daily relationship with Him.

Since that experience in October 2011, my desire to do the things I was excessively doing before has been completely extinguished! The things that were consuming all my time and energy were not sinful in themselves, but my level of doing them was akin to 'idolatry' and so God intervened in a big way to get my attention! And whilst He was at it, God revealed to me some areas of un-confessed and unrepentant sin that needed dealing with; hence my first book being written for the glory of God. A year later the Lord brought about the writing of my second book *The End of The World and What Jesus Has to Say About It*, which was published in 2014.

All I want to do until Jesus returns is to "be about my Father's business" (see Luke 2:49), and to do all of it for His glory. This is the only thing that matters to me now.

In between writing books, I am a housewife to my wonderful husband Chris, and a mother to my beautiful adult daughter, Emma. I am so thankful to the Lord that they both love and serve the Lord with their whole heart.

I enjoy the countryside, reading, photography, visiting teashops, and days out by the sea!

CONTACT THE AUTHOR

Follow Michele on Twitter: @MicheleNealUK

Visit her website: www.michelenealuk.com

Email Michele: info@michelenealuk.com

OTHER BOOKS BY THE AUTHOR

Come on Church! Wake Up! – Sin Within the Church and What Jesus Has to Say About It

Paperback:
ISBN 978-1-62136-316-3

e-book:
ISBN 978-1-62136-315-6

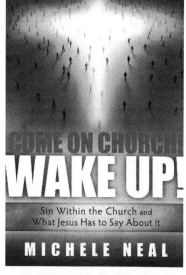

The End of The World and What Jesus Has to Say About It

Paperback:
ISBN 978-1-62136-742-0

e-book:
ISBN 978-1-62136-743-7

Both books available from Amazon, Barnes & Noble, and many other online book stores

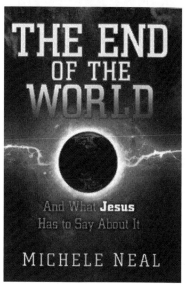

79583652R00078

Made in the USA
Columbia, SC
26 October 2017